MW00917348

Knowing and Doing the Will of God

David W. Jones

Veritas Publications

Copyright © 2017, 2019, 2021 David W. Jones
All rights reserved

Veritas Publications, Wake Forest, NC.

You may use brief quotations from this resource in books, articles, reviews, papers, and presentations. For all other uses, please contact Veritas Publications for permission. Email us at information@veritaspubs.com.

Unless otherwise noted, Scripture quotations are from the ESV® Bible (The Holy Bible, English Standard Version®), copyright © 2001 by Crossway, a publishing ministry of Good News Publishers. Used by permission. All rights reserved.

Scripture citations marked NKJV are from The New King James Version, copyright © 1979, 1980, 1982, Thomas Nelson, Inc., Publishers.

ISBN-10: 1521952655
ISBN-13: 978-1521952658

For the Church

CONTENTS

David W. Jones

PREFACE

Many years ago, an acquaintance approached me for marriage advice. In short, this friend, whom I'll call John, was considering proposing to his long-time girlfriend, whom I'll call Jennifer. As he explained it to me, John was a bit concerned about proposing to Jennifer, for, in his own words, he was less than sure that she was "the one." In talking with John, I came to learn that he had been taught in his church youth group that God has designated a specific spouse for each person to find and to marry—the elusive so-called "the one" in John's terminology. As John informed me, in his thinking the task of every unmarried Christian young person is to serve God faithfully, and to pray to God persistently, until God relents and supernaturally reveals "the one" whom we should marry. In short, according to my friend, finding and marrying this "the one" is God's will for our lives in regard to marriage.

The angst John was feeling, and the reason why he sought my counsel, was that he was not sure—again, in his own words—that he was properly "reading the signs" from God about Jennifer being "the one" for him. Furthermore, as he explained to me, John was concerned that if he incorrectly married Jennifer and she was not his "the one," then he would be simultaneously missing out on his "the one" and stealing someone else's "the one" in marriage. In essence, John's fear was that if he married the wrong girl he would be relegated to living a second-class Christian life (in regard to marriage, at least) and, as he explained it to me, he might even singlehandedly destroy

i

the entire institution of marriage via the cascade effect. A big concern, indeed!

In all honesty, I was a bit confused (and slightly entertained) by John's explanation of how, in his understanding, a young person should find a spouse. Having been raised in a different denomination than John, my theology of marriage varied from his mystical approach. As I explained to John, in my reading of Scripture, there is really only one inviolable rule regarding the selection of a spouse—that is, an unmarried Christian ought to marry another believer (see 2 Cor. 6:14). As Paul explained to the Corinthian church, if a Christian is unmarried and they desire to be married, then they are "free to be married to whom [they wish], only in the Lord" (1 Cor. 7:39). Obviously, common sense and wisdom are also important factors in such an important decision. Indeed, in his letter to the believers in Corinth, it is clear Paul assumed that a potential spouse is of the opposite gender and of the appropriate age to be married, presumably among many other practical concerns. Further, we are wise to marry someone to whom we are attracted, with whom we share similar interests, and the like.

To make a long story short, John and I had a number of lengthy meetings over several weeks. We talked about issues such as proper Bible interpretation, discerning God's will, the sufficiency of Scripture, and the institution of marriage. In the end, after making a few adjustments to his theology of marriage, John ended up proposing to Jennifer several months after our first meeting. You'll be happy to know she said, "Yes." As I write these words, John and Jennifer have been married for over a decade and have a house full of children. While they surely deal with the same challenges that every married couple faces, as far as I can tell, John and Jennifer have a happy marriage today.

I wish I could say that my conversation with John was a one-time event. However, as I've taught the Bible to God's people over the years, I've met many people who have a theology of God's will very similar to the model that John described to me. This is true not only in regard to marriage, but also concerning other life decisions, such as educational pursuits, vocational choices, and financial purchases, among the many other choices we face in life. When I embarked upon my career as a college and seminary professor, wanting to offer a correction to what I perceived to be a faulty model of knowing God's will, I designed a class entitled "Moral Decision Making and the Will of God." In this course I simply explain, as I did in my discussions with John, that the Bible is sufficient for Christian life and practice. As I've taught this class over parts of the past two decades, many students have asked me to put the material from the class into print, in an introductory primer-type format, so that they can share it with other believers in their families and in their churches. The book you hold in your hands is my answer to this request.

Before we begin our study, I need to give a brief word of caution and make a plea for grace and love. As I've taught on this topic over the years and in different settings, it has been my experience that some Christians will have an initial, emotional, adverse reaction to some of the material in this study for they will perceive it to be a personal attack on the way in which they have made life decisions in the past. This is especially true if you have been predisposed toward a mystical approach to knowing God's will. As you read this book, if you find yourself in this position, let me exhort you to keep reading and to hold both your present beliefs and the content of this book up to the light of Scripture. My intent in writing this book has not been to attack any other believer, nor to callously highlight biblical or theological errors. Rather, my goal has been to point the church toward the beauty, truth, and sufficiency of God's Word, which works continually to purify our theology. I trust you'll show me the same grace and love I have toward you as you read this book.

ACKNOWLEDGEMENTS

The Lord graciously called me into a relationship with Jesus Christ over thirty years ago. For most of my time as a follower of Christ, I've been privileged to be able to teach God's people the truths of His Word. As I think back through the many teaching opportunities I've had over the years, both in the church and in the academy, I believe I have had more discussions with fellow believers about God's will than any other topic. Sometimes these conversations have been very general (i.e., "How can I know God's will?"), other times they have been more specific in nature (i.e., "What is God's will in regard to bioethics?"). However, all of these discussions have been invaluable to me, as they have forced me to search the Scriptures and to think through the issues related to knowing and doing the will of God. Therefore, I want to thank all of the students with whom I've discussed the will of God over the years.

Furthermore, I am acutely aware that no publication is the work of one person. I have benefited from the input of many others while writing this manuscript. Indeed, there have been so many people who have helped me with this project, whether it be in the formal editing process, serving as proofreaders (any mistakes are still mine!), or discussing the contents of this book over a cup of coffee. As this project goes to print, I'd like to specially thank Dawn Jones, Billie Goodenough, Alan Bryan, Andrew Spencer, and Jeremy Bell for their valuable feedback, clarifying comments, and helpful edits.

David W. Jones

CHAPTER 1:
INTRODUCTION AND OVERVIEW

Browsing through the titles in a Christian bookstore, or conducting a simple Internet search, reveals that knowing God's will is a favorite topic among Christians. God's will is the subject of numerous books, articles, blog posts, and seminars each year. While the popularity of a topic is not always an accurate indicator of its importance, in regard to God's will the perennial interest believers have shown in this subject is indeed warranted, for the Bible teaches that Christian maturity is fundamentally tied to knowing and doing God's will. For example, Paul taught the Christians in Rome that the way to "not be conformed to this world . . . [is to] discern what is the will of God, what is good and acceptable and perfect" (Rom. 12:2). This process, writes Paul, entails a necessary renewal of the believer's mind.

Given the importance of this topic, it is not surprising to learn that there are almost fifty explicit references to God's will in the Bible, and there are hundreds of implied references. Yet, the prevalence of this theme in Scripture is not the only reason for its popularity. I believe another reason why knowing God's will is a topic of interest to Christians is that many people sense that God has a divine program for the world, which He is unfolding, and they genuinely want to be part of, and even help to facilitate, such a plan. Indeed, many believers have a desire to flourish spiritually and rightly believe that this is somehow tied to knowing and doing God's will. Yet, as this book will explain, Christians need to be sure that they have a correct conception of God's will and that they are seeking it properly. Such an orientation will enable Christians to identify the will of God and to keep it once it is found.

Perhaps another reason for the popularity of this topic is that Christians hear the testimony of others about the benefits of being in God's will and naturally desire the same for themselves. Moreover, many believers have simply been taught that seeking out and participating in God's will is an essential part of growing in Christian maturity, which is true. Indeed, Paul instructed the Thessalonian church, "For this is the will of God, your sanctification" (1 Thess. 4:3). It makes sense, then, to seek out the will of God. Furthermore, experience testifies that there is a certain spiritual and practical comfort in believing, or even knowing, that one is within God's will. Perhaps a desire for such an assurance is even one of the reasons why you're reading this book.

As we begin this study, we shouldn't overlook the fact that there can be some disingenuous, or even dangerous, reasons why some people seek out or appeal to the will of God. One such reason is that Western Christianity has been infected by the heresy of the prosperity gospel, which is no gospel at all. This false teaching connects the idea of being in God's will with material human flourishing. Since I've written at length about the prosperity gospel elsewhere,[1] we won't unpack the nuances and the extent of this false teaching here. To be sure, though, some immature or deceived believers seek out God's will because they selfishly desire health, wealth, and personal happiness, and they believe these things can be attained by finding the will of God. Those attracted to this heresy would do well to meditate upon Peter's arresting teaching that it may be the will of God that Jesus' followers unjustly suffer and die, even for doing good works (see 1 Pet. 3:17; 4:19).

Other related reasons why people may have an unhealthy interest in the will of God include: to appear spiritual, to cloak their own lust for power, or even to avoid accountability for past sins or otherwise bad decisions. Indeed, reasons such as these seem to have been present in Jeremiah's day, when royally appointed false prophets errantly taught that Jerusalem would not be destroyed. Through Jeremiah, God addressed these false teachers, as He declared, "Behold, I am against those who prophesy lying dreams, declares the LORD, and who tell them and lead my people astray by their lies and their recklessness, when I did not send them or charge them. So they do not profit this people at all, declares the LORD" (Jer. 23:32). A similar scenario is recorded in Job's interaction with his colleague Eliphaz the Temanite who claimed that his prideful accusations against Job were God's revealed will, although God later declared they were not (see Job 4:12–21; 42:7–8).

So, we must be aware of the sinful motives of some people who appeal to God's will—perhaps even ourselves, at times. Yet, since Jesus taught that we are to "will . . . to do God's will" (John 7:17), we must not be afraid of seeking God's will. Indeed, we must seek God's will and those in spiritual leadership ought to foster a desire for knowing and keeping God's will in the hearts and minds of those under their spiritual care. An important caveat, however, is that God's will must be rightly defined and properly sought. As we will explore in some detail in this book, most errors Christians make in regard to God's will do not relate to *whether* it should be sought, but rather *how* it should be sought. In other words, concerning the will of God, the most common errors believers make are not usually a matter of *essence*, but of *methodology*.

3

Being properly prepared to seek God's will is important, for the will of God relates to all aspects of life. Think of the possible areas of application for knowing and doing God's will. There are vocational issues such as where to attend school, what to study, obtaining employment, and ministerial callings. There are economic matters like major financial purchases, job opportunities, investing decisions, and charitable giving. There are also relationship issues such as when and whom to marry, the time for childbearing, and even end-of-life questions. And the list goes on. While not everyone will be faced with each of these choices, all believers will grapple with following God's will in certain areas of life. Indeed, if we define God's will as simply "God's desires for the world and the people who dwell in it," then there is no area of human existence in which the will of God would not be relevant.

Defining God's Will

While the preceding definition is an adequate working description of God's will, as we embark on this study it will be helpful if we first develop a more in-depth understanding of the concept of God's will. A survey of Scripture and Christian literature on the will of God reveals that there are three main categories or ways in which the term "God's will" (or a synonymous phrase) is commonly used. To elaborate, the concept is employed to refer to what could be termed God's sovereign will, God's moral will, and God's individual will. As our study progresses over the following chapters, we'll analyze each of these categories in order to determine whether or not they are biblically faithful. However, for the sake of furthering the present discussion, we'll briefly define these concepts below and then revisit the question of their biblical legitimacy later in this book, especially in chapters 3 and 4.

God's sovereign will refers to everything that God has eternally decreed.[2] The sovereign will of God can be thought of as God's master plan for the universe, and it includes everything that comes to pass. God's sovereign will cannot be known in advance (apart from prophecy) and it cannot be avoided once manifest. An Old Testament passage that encapsulates well the concept of God's sovereign will is Lam. 3:37–38, which reads, "Who has spoken and it came to pass, unless the Lord has commanded it? Is it not from the mouth of the Most High that good and bad come?" Similarly, in the New Testament, Jesus appealed to God's sovereign will when He taught, "Are not two sparrows sold for a penny? And not one of them will fall to the ground apart from [the will of] your Father" (Matt. 10:29). In fact, we can note that most of the passages in the Bible that reference God's will, whether explicitly or implicitly, have the category of God's sovereign will in view.

God's moral will is a second category and it refers to the moral standards that God has revealed to mankind, which He expects us to obey.[3] God's moral will is communicated in the Bible most clearly in His moral law. These moral standards apply to all areas of life and are the standard by which mankind is judged, for "sin is lawlessness" (1 John 3:4). Since God's moral will is not explicitly labeled as such in Scripture, in conceiving of the concept it may be helpful to think of passages such as the Ten Commandments (see Exod. 20:1–17; Deut. 5:1–22) or even Jesus' Sermon on the Mount (see Matthew 5–7).[4] As we keep the moral imperatives that are found in passages such as these, we functionally bear God's image, for God's moral laws reveal and reflect His own moral character and will. Since man is made in God's image, bearing God's image through keeping His moral law is fulfilling to man and pleasing to God. Observe Paul's instructions to the church in Colossae as he wrote that it is important to have "knowledge of [God's moral] will . . . so as to walk in a manner worthy of the Lord" (Col. 1:9–10).

God's individual will is the concept usually in view when Christians express a desire to find God's will. This is quite logical, for God's sovereign will is unknowable prior to its manifestation and His moral will is clear for everyone to read in Scripture. God's individual will can be thought of as a detailed and specific plan that God has for every believer. Many Christians believe this plan must be discovered and followed in order to flourish in the Christian life. Sometimes this idea is referred to by proponents of the concept as "being in the center of God's will." This aspect of God's will is the most debated of the three categories we've discussed, for it is difficult to find any explicit references to God's individual will in Scripture. This does not necessarily mean, however, that the concept is unbiblical. Indeed, if God is in control of all things, it seems reasonable to assume that He would have an individual plan for every believer to follow. We'll review advocates' evidence for an individual will of God in chapter 3 of this study.

As was previously noted, we can broadly define God's will as God's desires for the world and the people who dwell in it. Yet, when believers refer to the will of God, they often have in mind one of the three specific categories mentioned above: God's sovereign, moral, or individual wills. Sometimes, however, in common dialogue about God's will these three concepts can become blurred. This is understandable if we consider that these three categories of God's will may overlap. This can be conceived of if we picture three concentric circles, like an archery target. The innermost circle represents God's individual will, the next circle depicts God's moral will, and the outer circle symbolizes God's sovereign will. In such a diagram God's individual will is always contained within or overlaps with His moral will, which is always within or overlapping with His sovereign will. In light of this structure, then, in order to avoid confusion when talking about God's will, it is helpful to identify which specific concept is in view. We'll aim for such clarity in the ensuing discussion.

Preview of Contents

In the following chapters we'll study various aspects of the will of God, which hopefully will result in a clear understanding of how to know and to do God's will. Chapter 2 gives a biblical overview of God's will. In this chapter we'll look at various passages in Scripture that mention God's will, we'll review various pagan practices for seeking God's will, and we'll study different methodologies that God used in the Bible to reveal His will.

Chapter 3 contains an explanation of the most prevalent approach to knowing God's will in the modern church, which we'll label "the contemporary view." This chapter will examine this view, look at how it is practiced, show how it is argued, and cover some of the most significant critiques of this model that have been made—especially as this approach has gained popularity in the modern church.

Chapter 4 will examine and explain an alternative approach to knowing God's will, which we'll refer to as "the traditional view." This chapter will explain this view, examine how it is supported, look at how it relates to biblical wisdom and providence, and summarize some of the main emphases of this approach. This chapter will conclude by suggesting a practical model for knowing God's will and making moral decisions.

The purpose of chapter 5 is to go into more depth and to develop certain aspects of the model for knowing and doing God's will suggested in chapter 4. Specifically, this chapter will look at three topics that commonly arise in discussions about God's will. These topics are: prayer and moral decision making, the role of the Holy Spirit in knowing God's will, and navigating God's will in regard to Christian liberty.

The final chapter in this short book, which contains a conclusion and application, summarizes and synthesizes some of the important ideas contained in the previous four chapters. By giving a hypothetical example, this chapter also explores ways in which to teach and to apply one's view of knowing and doing God's will in the Christian community.

Summary Points

• The topic of the will of God is a perennial favorite of Christians, as many believers rightly understand that being in God's will is essential for Christian growth and discipleship.

• Some people pursue God's will for disingenuous reasons, such as to appear spiritual, to cloak their own lust for power, or to avoid accountability for past sins. We must be sure that our reasons for pursuing God's will are just.

• The concept of the sovereign will of God refers to everything that God has eternally decreed and it includes all things that come to pass. God's sovereign will cannot be known prior to its manifestation.

• The idea of God's moral will refers to the moral standards in the Bible that God has revealed to mankind. God's moral will can be equated with His moral law. To sin is to violate God's moral law.

• The category of God's individual will is the idea that God has a detailed and specific plan that every believer is to find and to follow. When many believers speak of finding God's will, they have God's individual will in view.

CHAPTER 2:
BIBLICAL EXAMPLES AND METHODOLOGIES

Historically speaking, knowing and doing the will of God, in the individualistic sense of the idea, was not a great concern for Christians. This may seem surprising at first, but consider the following: throughout history sons generally followed in their fathers' occupations, which was oftentimes maintaining the family farm, or worked in whatever trade was available; most daughters became wives and mothers once they were old enough to marry; schooling was limited and local; church attendance was expected and community-oriented; marriage, which entailed childbearing, was often arranged and limited in scope to those in one's immediate context; and most people didn't have disposable income or wide purchasing choices. It seems, then, that many of the issues about which contemporary believers seek God's individual will were a moot point for Christians in bygone eras. This helps explain why believers have historically emphasized *following* God's will, not *discovering* God's will.

Given that seeking God's individual will is a relatively recent phenomenon, then, it seems wise to ask if this endeavor is the result of recent cultural factors or if it is a legitimate biblical task. We'll move toward answering this question in the following chapter, yet for now we can observe that, indeed, God does promise to guide His followers in the Bible. For example, a well-known passage, Prov. 3:5–6, exhorts us, "Trust in the LORD with all your heart, and do not lean on your own understanding. In all your ways acknowledge him, and he will make straight your paths." Similarly, David records God's promise, "I will instruct you and teach you in the way you should go; I will counsel you with my eye upon you" (Ps. 32:8). Other passages that speak of God's will and His guidance of believers include Ps. 25:8–9, 12; 139:9–10; Prov. 20:24; Isa. 30:21; 58:11; and Rom. 8:14, among many others.

Beyond explicit references to God's leading of believers in Scripture there are many passages in which the idea of God's guidance is present and communicated via symbols, analogies, or word-pictures. For example, the Bible speaks of God as being a shepherd. Peter even refers to God as being the overseer and shepherd of believers' souls (see 1 Pet. 2:25). The role of a shepherd is to protect, to provide for, and to lead those whom he is over—namely, his sheep. Isaiah the prophet speaks of God's guidance in this context, writing, "He will tend his flock like a shepherd; he will gather the lambs in his arms; he will carry them in his bosom, and gently lead those that are with young" (Isa. 40:11). In a similar passage in the Gospel of John, in reference to His own ministry, Jesus taught, "The sheep hear his voice, and he calls his own sheep by name and leads them out. When he has brought out all his own, he goes before them, and the sheep follow him, for they know his voice" (John 10:3–4). Such verses create a very personal and tender picture of God's leadership of His saints.[1]

Another well-known analogy in the Bible that reveals the concept of God's guidance is the picture of God as a father. Of course, the role of a father is to protect, to provide for, and to lead his children. Perhaps the most well-known reference to God as a father in Scripture is in the so-called Lord's Prayer, where Jesus taught believers to pray, "Our Father in heaven, hallowed be your name. . . and lead us not into temptation, but deliver us from evil" (Matt. 6:9, 13). Another passage where God's guidance as a father is mentioned is Jer. 31:9. Here God speaks through Jeremiah and promises, "With weeping they shall come, and with pleas for mercy I will lead them back, I will make them walk by brooks of water, in a straight path in which they shall not stumble, for I am a father to Israel, and Ephraim is my firstborn."[2]

In light of the explicit references to God's guidance in Scripture, as well as the symbols, analogies, and word-pictures that God uses to reveal Himself, it is again worth repeating our earlier observation: The Lord *does* promise to guide His followers in His Word. Note, however, the verses cited above that reference God's guidance do not specify how He will guide nor do they explicitly mention the particular category of God's will that will be disclosed—sovereign, moral, or individual.

In the remainder of this chapter we'll investigate the various methodologies in Scripture through which God has chosen to reveal His will or by which men have sought to know God's will. As our survey will show, while it is always God's prerogative to reveal His will and to give guidance supernaturally, the occasions by which God chose to do so in an individualistic sense are not as common as one might think. Moreover, as we'll see in the following section, men have sometimes endeavored to seek divine guidance in illegitimate ways.

Pagan Methodologies

Before we study the valid ways in which God was pleased to reveal His will in the Bible, we will briefly look at a number of pagan methodologies of divination—or, at least, attempts at divination. These practices are covered here in this chapter for they are "biblical," in the sense of being described in the Bible; yet none of these methodologies are legitimate for followers of Jesus Christ, for Scripture repeatedly condemns pagan practices of divination.[3]

False Prophets

One of the most common ways in Scripture by which pagans sought to know the will of God is through turning to false prophets. In any context the presence of false prophets can be dangerous, for they can be confused—sometimes willfully so—with true prophets. Indeed, God clearly warned His people about the hazards of following false prophets, even telling them that some false prophets may be able to perform signs and wonders.[4] Yet, Scripture teaches that such events were merely a test of God's people's allegiance to the Lord (see Deut. 13:1–3).

In spite of God's warnings, false prophets abound in the narrative of Scripture, and they frequently deceive God's people. Major examples of false prophets include the four hundred men in Ahab's court (see 1 Kings 22:6–12), those in Jerusalem who deceived the people about their coming exile (see Jer. 23:25–32; Ezek. 13:1–9), and the prophets who attempted to discourage Nehemiah from rebuilding the city wall (see Neh. 6:10–14). There are many other examples of false prophets in both Old and New Testaments. Given the prevalence of false prophets in the Bible, it seems likely that we should expect an equal presence of false prophets today working among those who claim the name of Christ. Indeed, Paul taught that men will always desire to "accumulate for themselves [false] teachers to suit their own passions" (2 Tim. 4:3) and Jude warns the universal church about apostasy in the end-times (see Jude 3–19).[5]

Casting of Lots

Another pagan methodology of divination in Scripture is the casting of lots. As with the appeal to false prophets, so the casting of lots can be confusing for believers, for there are legitimate instances of lot-casting in Scripture (see the discussion later in this chapter). Examples of lot-casting by pagans include Haman's attempt to decipher a day on which to exterminate the Jews (see Est. 3:7; 9:24), the pagan nations' casting of lots to divide God's people in exile (see Joel 3:3), and the Roman soldiers' casting of lots to determine who would get Jesus' garments at His crucifixion (see Matt. 27:35).[6] These passages don't explain the nuances of lot-casting; however, most scholars believe the practice was similar to the children's game known as "pick-up sticks" or "choose the shortest straw."[7]

Rhabdomancy, Teraphim, and Hepatoscopy

An important verse in our review of pagan practices of divination is Ezek. 21:21, which reads, "For the king of Babylon stands at the parting of the way, at the head of the two ways, to use divination. He shakes the arrows; he consults the teraphim; he looks at the liver." This verse is interesting, for it records three different means of divination used by Nebuchadnezzar as he attempted to discern the correct path for his conquering army. First, this passage mentions rhabdomancy, which is the use of arrows to determine the will of God. This methodology is also referenced at 2 Kings 13:15–19 and may be alluded to at 1 Sam. 20:20–22. Second, this verse says that the king "consults the teraphim." Teraphim were family or tribal idols that some pagans believed would provide guidance and give protection. An example of such household gods in Scripture were the idols that Rachel stole from Laban as is recorded at Gen. 31:19.[8] Third, this passage mentions the practice of hepatoscopy, which is the study of the liver of a dead animal in order to discern the will of God. Note

13

that hepatoscopy is only mentioned here in Scripture but is still practiced in some animistic religions today.

Oneiromancy

Another pagan methodology of divination is oneiromancy, which is the interpretation of dreams and visions to determine the will of God (see Deut. 13:1–3; Jer. 29:8–9; Jude 1:8). As with the consultation of prophets and the casting of lots, so learning God's will via dreams and visions can be a confusing concept for Christians, for in the Bible God occasionally used dreams and visions to communicate His will to His people. We'll study the legitimate use of dreams and visions in Scripture later in this chapter. While oneiromancy is generally only seen today among occultists and some charismatic groups, all believers must be sure they correctly view the practice, for God declares, "Behold, I am against those who prophesy lying dreams, declares the LORD, and who tell them and lead my people astray by their lies and their recklessness, when I did not send them or charge them. So they do not profit this people at all, declares the LORD" (Jer. 23:32). Indeed, oneiromancy must be understood—and the pagan form of it rejected—lest we give God a cause to set Himself against us for pursuing lying dreams and visions.

Hydromancy

Among the other pagan methodologies of divination described in the Bible is the practice of hydromancy, which is the use of water (or another liquid, such as wine or even blood) to determine the will of God. This practice is referred to in the biblical narrative when Joseph accused his brothers of stealing his silver cup, which Joseph had directed his steward to hide in Benjamin's sack of grain. When the steward confronted Joseph's brothers, he claimed that Joseph used the silver cup to practice hydromancy (see Gen. 44:1–5). Joseph later reiterated this claim himself (see Gen. 44:15); however, it is unclear whether or not Joseph actually practiced hydromancy or if this was just part of Joseph's attempt to conceal his identity from his brothers.

Necromancy

Another pagan methodology of divination that appears in Scripture is necromancy. This is the practice of consulting the dead in an attempt to learn God's will. Regarding necromancy, God warned His people, "Do not turn to mediums or necromancers; do not seek them out, and so make yourselves unclean by them: I am the LORD your God" (Lev. 19:31; see Deut. 18:10–12; 26:14; Isa. 8:19). In spite of this warning, King Saul foolishly consulted a medium in an attempt to commune with the deceased prophet Samuel (see 1 Sam. 28:3–25).[9] The Bible teaches that Saul's necromancy was one of the reasons for his own death, which occurred at the initiative of God (see 1 Chron. 10:13).[10]

Astrology

A final methodology of divination that appears in Scripture is astrology, which is the consultation of heavenly bodies to discern the will of God. An example of this can be seen at 2 Kings 23:5, which refers to "the priests . . . [who] make offerings in the high places at the cities of Judah and around Jerusalem . . . to the sun and the moon and the constellations and all the host of the heavens." Other biblical references to astrology include Isa. 47:13–14; Dan. 2:27–28; 4:7. In an organized religious sense, this practice is not as prevalent in contemporary Western culture as it was in ancient times,[11] yet astrology can be seen in peoples' reading of newspaper horoscopes and is still formally practiced within the occult.

Clearly, pagan methodologies of divination are wide-ranging in the Bible. A commonality between the various practices cited above is that they were not commanded by God. In fact, as was noted, many of these methodologies were explicitly prohibited by God. Further, individuals who engaged in pagan divination in Scripture are not lauded for their actions, generally received no guidance, and were often condemned (or even killed) by God for their pagan practices. In the following section, we'll turn to a survey of a number of legitimate biblical methodologies by which God chose to reveal His will to His people.

Biblical Methodologies

As was previously noted, the various pagan methodologies of divination that appear in Scripture are "biblical" in the sense of being found in the Bible; however, they are not valid for followers of Christ. In the present section we'll survey a number of truly biblical methodologies by which God was pleased to reveal His will in Scripture and to give guidance to His followers. We'll use the term *biblical methodologies* to describe these practices, for these means are both found in the Bible and were utilized by God. In the ensuing discussion we'll describe and analyze each biblical methodology and briefly consider the viability of these practices in the modern context. Later, in chapter 3, we'll engage in a more in-depth discussion of whether or not these biblical methodologies are repeatable or valid for contemporary believers.

The Created Order

The broadest and most general way in which God reveals Himself, including His will, is through the created order. Theologians call this methodology "general revelation" and speak of it as having two main parts: the external witness of the creation and the internal witness of the conscience.[12] Scripture often mentions the revelation of God in the created order.[13] For example, in the Psalms David writes of the knowledge of God available in creation as he proclaims, "The heavens declare the glory of God, and the sky above proclaims his handiwork. Day to day pours out speech, and night to night reveals knowledge. There is no speech, nor are there words, whose voice is not heard. Their voice goes out through all the earth, and their words to the end of the world" (Ps. 19:1–4). Similarly, in his letter to the Romans, Paul writes of the created order and the moral accountability of all men, noting that "their conscience also bears witness [to God], and their conflicting thoughts accuse or even excuse them" (Rom. 2:15).

As these passages teach, God reveals Himself to mankind via the created order as He pours out His speech and stirs man's conscience to conviction. Admittedly though, experience teaches that such revelation can seem imprecise. Yet, we dare not question the substance of what is revealed via the created order, for in Paul's extended discussion of general revelation he notes that what is revealed is "truth" (Rom. 1:18, 25) that may be "known" (Rom. 1:19, 21), "perceived" (Rom. 1:20), and "understood" (Rom. 1:20). In this same passage, however, Paul also teaches that this revelation may be "suppressed" (Rom. 1:18). Given this fact, as well as the hardness of man's heart, we may justly question the helpfulness of the created order in revealing God's will, especially in regard to specific instances of divine guidance. This highlights believers' need for the special revelation of the Word of God.

True Prophets

Another biblical methodology by which God communicated His will in Scripture is through true prophets. This means of revelation is arguably the most common way in which God gave guidance in the Old Testament, as the majority of the books of the Old Testament were written by a prophet, with many being named after a prophet. The New Testament, too, contains occasional references to prophets (see Luke 2:36; Acts 11:28; 21:9–10).[14] In fact, in the entire Bible there are more than fifty named prophets and prophetesses, seven specific unnamed prophets, and numerous general references to prophets and prophetesses.

Observe that the ministry of prophets is fairly wide-ranging in Scripture. A commonality among all of the prophets is that they were called by God in order to deliver specific, oftentimes detailed, revelation from God to mankind. As was noted in our review of pagan methodologies, false prophets also abounded in biblical times. Therefore, God gave His people two tests by which they could discern a true prophet from a false prophet— first, they could compare the words of a prophet with what had been previously recorded in Scripture (see Deut. 13:1–3); and second, they could monitor if a prophet's words were actually fulfilled (see Deut. 18:20–22). Failure at either one of these tests was a sure sign of false prophecy, while passing both tests might—but not necessarily— signal the presence of a true prophet.

Many prophets exercised a long and fruitful ministry and served the Lord well. However, given the possibility for confusion between true and false prophets, this means of knowing God's will was challenging, at best. Moreover, prophets had to wait to receive a word from the Lord (see 1 Sam. 3:1; 1 Kings 18:1; Jer. 42:7). In other words, during much of the biblical era, God's people did not have direct access to the Word of God apart from Him sending it through a prophet. At Amos 8:11 God even taught that because of the people's bent toward disobedience, there would occasionally be times of "a famine . . . of hearing the words of the LORD." In contrast to this, modern believers can rejoice at the teaching of the author of the book of Hebrews who wrote, "Long ago, at many times and in many ways, God spoke to our fathers by the prophets, but in these last days he has spoken to us by his

Son, whom he appointed the heir of all things, through whom also he created the world" (Heb. 1:1–2). Indeed, the knowledge of Christ available in the Bible is a more sure and consistent Word from God than that brought by the prophets.

Urim and Thummim

One of the most obscure methodologies of the revelation of God's will in Scripture is the Urim and Thummim. This practice (or, perhaps, device) is first mentioned by God, without explanation, at Exod. 28:30 as He gave Moses instructions for making the priestly garments to be used in the Tabernacle. Given the passing nature of this first reference, it seems that the Urim and Thummim were well-known to Moses and to the people prior to this time. The Urim and Thummim are explicitly mentioned only seven additional times in the Bible, with there being a few occasions in Scripture where the Urim and Thummim may have been present, although they are not explicitly named (see Judg. 1:1; 20:18, 23; 1 Sam. 30:7–8). The Urim and Thummim were used most frequently between the time of the Exodus event and the time of David. Since the beginning of the monarchy entailed the proliferation of prophets in Israel, it seems that as the prophetic office rose in prominence, so the use of the Urim and Thummim declined.

Scholars are not in agreement as to exactly what the Urim and Thummim were or how they functioned. This is due to the lack of information in the Bible about this methodology and the fact that there are no detailed examples of the use of the Urim and Thummim in Scripture.[15] Some have suggested that the Urim and Thummim were square stones that could be rolled like dice in order to determine God's will. Others have proposed that the Urim and Thummim were sacred lots that could be cast before the Lord in order to get divine guidance (see the following section on lot-casting). Since the words "Urim" and "Thummim" are likely derived from the Hebrew terms for "light" and "perfection," the ancient historian Josephus suggested that Urim and Thummim was merely a phrase used to describe the twelve tribal stones on the high priest's ephod, which he proposed might supernaturally glow in order to indicate the will of God.

However trivial or fanciful some of the above suggestions might seem, none of these ideas should be ruled out without consideration. Yet, I believe a more likely identification for the Urim and Thummim is that it was simply a design component of the high priest's ephod, or breastplate, which symbolized his authority to serve as a mediator between man and God, including his unique role of delivering divine communication. Note that the Urim and Thummim are exclusively mentioned in Scripture in conjunction with the priesthood and were undoubtedly connected to the functions of the high priest in his mediatorial role (see Num. 27:21; Deut. 33:8; Ezra 2:63; Neh. 7:65).[16] Two times in Scripture God instructs His people to keep the Urim and Thummim in or on the high priest's ephod, specifying that "they shall be on Aaron's heart, when he goes in before the LORD" (Exod. 28:30; see Lev. 8:8). By way of analogy, we can say that just as the Decalogue was placed within the Holy of Holies, so the Urim and Thummim were placed within the high priest's breastplate. It may be the case that just as the Decalogue revealed God's moral will to His people, so the Urim and Thummim revealed the light and perfection of God's will through the ministry of the high priest.[17]

In any event, we ought not to be too dogmatic about our identification of the Urim and Thummim, for there is simply not enough information in the Bible to reach an absolute conclusion. However, we can definitively say that the use of the Urim and Thummim fell out of practice with God's people many centuries before the time of

Christ. Thus, we ought not to expect the Urim and Thummim, whatever the practice (or device) may have been, to be utilized by contemporary believers in knowing and doing the will of God.

Casting of Lots

In our review of pagan methodologies of divination in Scripture we noted that pagans occasionally cast lots in an attempt to gain divine guidance. While lot-casting was not a widespread practice among God's people, it was nevertheless utilized and accepted (or, at least, accommodated) by God. As we discussed earlier, Scripture is not clear in regard to the exact details of the practice of lot-casting—either by pagans or by God's people. However, the Bible does teach that lot-casting was invoked by God's people for tasks such as allotment of land (see Num. 26:55; Josh. 14:2; 18:6, 10), choosing of a king (see 1 Sam. 10:20–21), determination of judicial guilt (see Josh. 7:14–18; 1 Sam. 14:41–42), assignment of dwelling places (see Neh. 11:1), division of priestly service (see 1 Chron. 26:13; Neh. 10:34), choice of the scape-goat on the Day of Atonement (see Lev. 16:8–9), and even the election of an apostle (see Acts 1:26).

Upon reviewing the examples of lot-casting in Scripture, it seems that lots were used in two related yet separate ways. First, lots were used by God's people to make an impartial choice between otherwise equal options. Examples of such usage include the division of land by Joshua, the choice of the scape-goat by the high priest, and Nehemiah's determination of whom among the returning exiles would be chosen to dwell in Jerusalem. Second, lot-casting was employed in order to discern the will of God and to get supernatural guidance in certain contexts. Examples of such divine direction include the choice of Saul to be the first Israelite king, the identification of Jonathan as the one who had violated Saul's prescribed fast, and the choice of Matthias as an apostle to replace Judas.

Considering the practice of lot-casting as a whole, it seems unlikely that this biblical methodology—as least in its supernatural sense—could be effectively utilized by the modern church in order to discern the will of God. Although the casting of lots was practiced by God's people in Scripture, there are no instructions in the Bible regarding how to cast lots, nor are there any instances of the lot being used by believers after the establishment of the church. Moreover, every instance of lot-casting in Scripture was facilitated by a prophet, priest, or apostle. In light of these facts, it seems that the casting of lots—again, in the supernatural sense—ought not to be viewed as a valid practice for contemporary believers.[18]

Dreams and Visions

Earlier, in our survey of pagan divination, we briefly reviewed the practice of oneiromancy, which is the interpretation of dreams and visions in an attempt to gain divine guidance. In Scripture God repeatedly warned his people about oneiromancy in verses such as Jer. 29:8, which reads, "Do not listen to the dreams that [false prophets] dream." Nevertheless, God did use dreams and visions in the Bible to communicate truth to His people— although this happened quite rarely. In fact, in the thousands of years of history recorded in the Bible, there are less than thirty individuals who received dreams or visions from God. In the Old Testament, major examples include Joseph (see Gen. 37:5–11), Nebuchadnezzar (see Dan. 2:1–45; 4:1–27), and Daniel (see Dan. 7:1–8:27). In the New Testament, only a few individuals are recorded as having had dreams or visions, including: Joseph (see Matt. 1:20–21; 2:13), Paul (see Acts 16:6–10; 22:17–21), Cornelius (see Acts 10:3–6), and Peter (see Acts 10:9–15).[19]

So, although it wasn't common, God did use dreams

and visions in times past to give guidance to His people. However, this methodology seems to be an unlikely (and, perhaps, even undesirable) means of revelation for contemporary believers. Consider the following observations. First, in the biblical era, dreams and visions were not sought by any of the limited number of individuals who received them, nor are God's people ever exhorted to seek dreams or visions as a means of revelation. Rather, in Scripture, dreams and visions came spontaneously from God to those who experienced them. Further, the majority of individuals who received a dream or a vision experienced it as a one-time event, not as a recurring pattern of divine guidance. In fact, in the Bible it seems those who had multiple dreams of divine origin, such as Joseph and Daniel, received the same information in various forms via several different dreams.

Second, most of the dreams and visions experienced in the Bible were vague in nature, highly symbolic, and required special interpretation for understanding.[20] Examples include Joseph's dreams of sheaves and celestial bodies (see Gen. 37:5–11), Pharaoh's dream about bundles of grain and livestock (see Gen. 41:1–36), and an unnamed Midianite soldier's dream of a tumbling loaf of barley bread (see Judg. 7:13). Moreover, that which is revealed in Scripture via dreams and visions is often negative or undesirable, including the threat to Abimelech's life because he took Sarah as a wife (see Gen. 20:3–7), the impending death of Pharaoh's chief baker (see Gen. 40:16–19), and Joseph's immediate need to flee the country on account of Herod's intent to kill his son, Jesus (see Matt. 2:13).

In sum, then, although there is certainly a veneer of spirituality to the idea of receiving divine guidance via dreams and visions, upon considering the biblical narrative it becomes clear that this methodology was never widely used by God. Further, it should not be overlooked that many of the dreams and visions in Scripture, which were legitimate means of revelation, were received by unbelievers. Therefore, in light of the vague nature and often adverse message of dreams and visions in Scripture, it seems unlikely that this biblical methodology will be helpful to modern believers in seeking to know and to do the will of God (see Eccl. 5:7).

Angelic Visitation

Another biblical methodology of divine communication is angelic visitation. The writer of the book of Hebrews teaches that angels are "ministering spirits sent out to serve for the sake of those who are to inherit salvation" (Heb. 1:14). Scripture records several instances where the ministry of angels included visits with mankind. Notable individuals in the Old Testament who encountered angels include: Abraham (see Gen. 18:2), Moses (see Exod. 3:1–10), Elijah (see 1 Kings 19:5), and Daniel (see Dan. 9:20–27).[21] There are fewer appearances of angels in the New Testament, with most occasions being in the Gospels or the book of Acts. Those who were visited by angels in the New Testament include: Mary (see Luke 1:26–38), Joseph (see Matt. 1:20–21), Peter (see Acts 12:7–11), and Paul (see Acts 27:23).[22]

A survey of the instances of angelic visitation in Scripture reveals that the purpose of these supernatural encounters was often related to physical or material provision in a time of need. For example, angels brought food to Elijah when he fled from Jezebel (see 1 Kings 19:5); angels attended to Jesus after His temptation (see Matt. 4:11); angels ministered to Christ before His crucifixion (see Luke 22:43); an angel rescued the apostles from prison (see Acts 5:19); an angel delivered Peter from his incarceration (see Acts 12:7–11); and an angel encouraged Paul regarding his deliverance during a storm at sea (see Acts 27:23). Clearly, serving mankind in times of distress is an important part of the angels' ministry.

Indeed, in the Psalms, David praises God for the angels' ministry to mankind as he writes, "Bless the LORD, all his hosts, his ministers, who do his will!" (Ps. 103:21).

Of more interest to this study, however, is the observation that in the Bible angelic visitation often entailed delivering information from God to mankind about God's will, including information about future events. These angelic visits often occurred in conjunction with the birth of key individuals in the biblical narrative. For example, an angel announced the impending birth of Abraham's son Ishmael to Hagar (see Gen. 16:11); the angel Gabriel announced the imminent conception of John the Baptist to his father Zacharias (see Luke 1:11–20); Gabriel announced the impending conception of Jesus to Mary (see Luke 1:26–38); and an angel announced the birth of Jesus to the shepherds who were in the fields surrounding Bethlehem, saying, "For unto you is born this day in the city of David a Savior, who is Christ the Lord" (Luke 2:11).[23]

Another way in which angels gave divine guidance to God's people was in combination with the aforementioned practice of oneiromancy. On at least five occasions in Scripture individuals had dreams or visions that required angelic interpretation for understanding. This occurred most frequently with Daniel, as he needed angelic interpretation to understand his vision of a ram and a goat (see Dan. 8:16–26), his vision of the so-called seventy weeks prophecy, which was interpreted by the angel Gabriel (see Dan. 9:21–27), and his vision of a glorious man (see Dan. 10:1–12:9). In addition to Daniel, the prophet Zechariah required an angelic visit to understand his obscure vision of a horseman and four horses (see Zech. 1:9–11), and the apostle John received divine guidance from an angel as he sought to understand his visions recorded in the book of Revelation (see Rev. 1:1; 17:7–18; 22:16).[24]

A final way in which angels provided divine guidance in the Bible is by communicating specific directions from God to mankind. For instance, as was mentioned earlier in our review of dreams and visions, an angel appeared to Joseph in a dream and instructed him to flee to Egypt on account of Herod's intent to kill Jesus (see Matt. 2:13). This same angel later commanded Joseph to return to Israel after the death of Herod (see Matt. 2:19–20). In the book of Acts there are several examples of angelic visitation that included specific guidance, including an angel instructing the apostles to teach in the Temple (see Acts 5:19–20), an angel directing Philip toward his encounter with the Ethiopian eunuch (see Acts 8:26), and an angel instructing Cornelius to send men to Joppa in order to arrange for a visit with Peter (see Acts 10:3–5).

As with many of the other biblical methodologies we've studied in this chapter, angelic encounters seem to be an unlikely way for those in the modern church to receive regular divine guidance. Perhaps the greatest reason why this is so is the infrequency of angelic visits in the Bible. Scripture records less than two dozen individuals who experienced this phenomenon, the majority of whom lived in the Old Testament era and all of whom did not seek an audience with the angels whom they encountered. Furthermore, when angelic visitation did occur in the Bible, the reaction of the individuals involved was oftentimes one of fear and angst. For instance, when Daniel was visited by the angel Gabriel he testified, "I was frightened and fell on my face" (Dan. 8:17). Moreover, the apostle John inappropriately attempted to worship angels on two different occasions due to the overwhelming nature of angelic visitation (see Rev. 19:10; 22:8).

We should also note that some of the angelic visitations in Scripture were for the purpose of meting out divine judgment or delivering troubling news. This ought to quell many people's desire for an angelic encounter. Examples in the Bible when angels delivered divine judgment or otherwise bad news include: the two angels who visited Lot before destroying Sodom and Gomorrah (see Gen. 19:1–29), the angel who killed 185,000 Assyrian soldiers encamped around Jerusalem (see 2 Kings 19:35), the angel who was preparing to destroy Jerusalem because of David's sin of taking a census (see 2 Sam. 24:16–17), and the angels in the book of Revelation who will carry out God's judgment upon the earth via the blowing of trumpets, the breaking of seals, and the pouring out of bowls of divine wrath (see Rev. 8:1–9:21; 11:15–19; 16:1–21).

In summary, then, given the infrequency of angelic visitation in the Bible, the fact that Christians are never commanded to seek such occurrences, the sometimes frightening nature of angelic encounters, and angels' role as bearers of divine judgment, it seems this biblical methodology of revealing God's will is an improbable (if not, undesirable) event today. Yet, in spite of the unlikelihood of angelic encounters, believers would be wise to heed the words of the author of the book of Hebrews who exhorted the church, "Do not neglect to show hospitality to strangers, for thereby some have entertained angels unawares" (Heb. 13:2).[25]

Supernatural Signs

A final biblical methodology used by God to disclose His will to mankind is supernatural signs. Supernatural signs, which usually can be categorized as miracles, are not common in the Bible; yet, on account of their phenomenal nature, they tend to attract our attention. While all supernatural signs reflect or communicate God's will—in the sense of being facilitated by God—not all of the supernatural events in Scripture occurred for the purpose of providing individual guidance. For example, many of the miracles Jesus performed, such as His walking on the Sea of Galilee (see Matt. 14:22–33) and His cursing of the fig tree (see Mark 11:12–14, 20–24), were performed to communicate His deity or to reflect the essence of the gospel, not for the sake of giving personal guidance.

However, some of the supernatural signs recorded in Scripture *did* occur for the purpose of giving divine guidance to God's people. For example, God appeared to Moses in the burning bush, which was not consumed, for the purpose of directing Moses to lead the Israelites out of bondage in Egypt (see Exod. 3:1–22). Similarly, during the exodus event God went before His people as a miraculous pillar of cloud by day and pillar of fire by night in order "to lead them along the way" (Exod. 13:21). Other examples of supernatural signs in Scripture that God used to reveal His will or to guide His people include handwriting on the palace wall of Babylon (see Dan. 5:1–29), the speaking of Balaam's donkey (see Num. 22:22–35), and the bright light and voice Paul heard on the road to Damascus (see Acts 9:1–9). Observe that many of the supernatural signs in the Bible occurred in connection with other means of revelation such as the appearance of an angel, the presence of a prophet, or a divine voice from heaven.

In biblical discussions about knowing and doing the will of God, the most often cited supernatural sign is likely the narrative of Gideon's fleece, which is recorded in Judg. 6:36–40. The details of this account are well-known by most Christians: in order to confirm that he would deliver the Israelites from Midianite oppression, Gideon tested God on successive evenings by putting out a fleece. Gideon first asked that the fleece be wet and the ground remain dry, and then that the ground be wet and the fleece remain dry. God graciously accommodated both of Gideon's requests, thus confirming to Gideon his place as Israel's deliverer. Some believers view Gideon's example as a blueprint to be followed as they metaphorically "put out a fleece," via some contrived test, in order to discern the will of God. This has become popular, in part, for this is one of a very few supernatural signs in Scripture that was asked for by a man and accommodated by God.[26] Yet, are Gideon's actions a model for us to follow? Keep reading.

As with many of the other biblical methodologies we've surveyed in this chapter, supernatural signs seem unlikely to benefit modern believers who desire to know and to do God's will. This is due simply to their infrequency of occurrence. Indeed, what distinguishes supernatural signs in the narrative of Scripture is their rarity. Given that there are only a handful of individuals who received supernatural signs in the Bible, it seems that most modern believers will never witness a supernatural sign, let alone have such revelation regularly. Additionally, it is clear that very few biblical characters asked God for the signs they did receive,[27] and Scripture nowhere commands believers to seek supernatural signs.

Jesus' teaching on supernatural signs is worth noting. In his Gospel Matthew reports that after Jesus had publicly healed a man who was demon-possessed, blind, and mute, the Pharisees asked Christ for another supernatural sign. Jesus responded, "An evil and adulterous generation seeks for a sign, but no sign will be given to it except the sign of the prophet Jonah" (Matt. 12:39; see Matt. 16:1–4). It seems that Jesus' refusal to accommodate the Pharisees' request was related to their rejection of His previous works and teachings.[28] This connection between unbelief and supernatural signs can also be seen in the aforementioned account of Gideon's fleece. In the Gideon narrative it is clear that God had already explicitly revealed His will to Gideon (see Judg. 6:11–27), which entailed Gideon delivering the Israelites from Midianite oppressors. Yet, because of Gideon's *unbelief* he asked God for a supernatural sign. Although God graciously consented, it is evident that Gideon's request for a sign was born out of doubt and spiritual immaturity—it was not a demonstration of his faith.

Conclusion

After reviewing various pagan methodologies of divination and several biblical methodologies of revelation in this chapter, we can conclude that specific and direct revelations of God's will apart from Scripture are not common. While extraordinary revelations from God did occasionally occur in the millennia of time covered by Scripture, their appearance is so rare that these events cannot be considered normative. The infrequency of these occurrences, coupled with the vague nature of what was often revealed, leaves us asking how best to get divine guidance. In the following chapters we'll look at two different models that have been proposed by Christians to assist us in knowing and doing the will of God.

Summary Points

• In the Bible God does promise to lead and to guide His people. This promise is stated in several passages and is also communicated in Scripture via a number of symbols, analogies, and word-pictures.

• In Scripture God explicitly condemns and gives warnings about many pagan methodologies of divination, such as false prophets, the use of dreams and visions, and astrology, among other practices.

• Throughout the Bible God chose to reveal Himself to mankind through various methodologies, including the created order, true prophets, the casting of lots, Urim and Thummim, dreams and visions, angelic appearances, and supernatural signs.

• It is God's prerogative to reveal Himself in any manner He so chooses; however, God very rarely uses extraordinary means of revelation such as angelic appearances, prophetic messages, supernatural signs, and the like.

• Given the infrequency of most of the biblical

methodologies of the revelation of God's will, it seems unlikely that pursuing such events will help modern Christians seeking explicit divine guidance and knowledge of an individual will of God.

CHAPTER 3:
THE CONTEMPORARY VIEW

From our survey of biblical examples and methodologies in the previous chapter, two observations about knowing God's will come to light. First, in the Bible God *does* promise to reveal His will and to give guidance to His people. We saw this in passages such as Ps. 32:8; Prov. 3:5–6; and Isa. 40:11, among several other verses that were cited. Second, as was noted at the conclusion of the previous chapter, contemporary Christians should not expect to regularly receive explicit, personal, extraordinary revelations from God and extra-biblical guidance. This is so because Scripture reports that even among biblical characters such events were infrequent, often vague, easy to confuse with pagan divination, and—perhaps most importantly—never commanded to be sought. Of course, this is not a commentary on what God *can* do in our world, but rather is a summary of what God *did* do in Scripture.

Given that God does promise to reveal His will, yet extraordinary revelations are not normative, many believers are naturally left wondering how best to obtain divine guidance. In order to address this conundrum, several views or models of knowing God's will have been suggested by well-meaning Christians. One such view that has been proposed, which we'll explore and analyze in this chapter, can be called the contemporary view.[1] This perspective, which is assumed by many in the church today, begins with the idea that there is a detailed, secret, individual will of God for every believer. This divine will relates to all areas of one's life and, according to its proponents, is especially important to follow in regard to major life decisions. Advocates of the contemporary view teach that since an individual will of God for Christians is presently hidden and unknown, it must be discovered over time by every believer in order to progress in spiritual maturity and to flourishing in the Christian life.[2] Several pieces of evidence have been suggested in support of this model.

Evidence for the Contemporary View

The evidence most often cited in support of the contemporary view is simply the many verses already mentioned in the first two chapters of this study that reference God's will, either explicitly or implicitly. In other words, since the contemporary view begins with the presupposition that there is a specific will of God for every believer, which is currently hidden, when advocates of this position read the many passages in Scripture that ambiguously mention God's will, they often assume that an individual will of God is in view. So, for example, when advocates of this model read Jesus' teaching at Mark 3:35, "For whoever does the will of God, he is my brother and sister and mother," they assume that Jesus is referring to an individual will of God. According to proponents of the contemporary view, finding and following this secret, individual will of God is of the utmost importance, for happiness and success in Christian living is at stake.

As was noted in chapter one of this book, assuming that biblical allusions to God's will are references to an individual will of God for each believer may be a tenuous proposition. Many scholars believe that passages used to support the idea of an individual will of God are better categorized as references to God's sovereign will or to God's moral will. Yet, perhaps counterintuitively, this leads to another piece of evidence suggested by proponents of the contemporary view—that is, advocates of this model argue that since God clearly does have a moral will and a sovereign will, it is both logical and reasonable to assume that God has an individual will for every believer to find and to follow. Indeed, given the existence of God's moral and sovereign wills, as well as His expressed desire for an intimate relationship with mankind, the assumption that God has an individual will for every believer can be viewed as a rational (although not necessary) deduction.

A final piece of evidence offered in support of the contemporary view comes from biblical and personal examples. Such examples are likely the most frequently cited type of arguments given in favor of this model of discerning God's will. Certainly those who regularly gather with the church have heard personal testimonies from other Christians about being in the center of God's will and the peace they've found therein. Moreover, it seems that many biblical characters had the experience of discovering an individual will of God. For example, Jesus testified, "My food is to do the will of him who sent me and to accomplish his work" (John 4:34). Similarly, the Holy Spirit directed the church at Antioch, "Set apart for me Barnabas and Saul for the work to which I have called them" (Acts 13:2). Other examples of God's individual will playing out in the lives of biblical characters include Philip, who was specifically sent to share the gospel with the Ethiopian eunuch, Ananias who was individually directed to visit Paul after his Damascus road experience, and Peter who was personally sent to preach to Cornelius and to his entire household. In each of these examples it seems that the biblical characters learned, were instructed in, and followed God's individual will for their lives.

Practice of the Contemporary View

Although the evidence offered in favor of the contemporary view may seem to be circumstantial to some, for others it is convincing and justifies a perspective that presents a viable answer to the question of how believers can receive divine guidance and flourish in the Christian life. Obviously, in order to use this model, advocates need a way to receive information about God's individual will for their lives. By way of actual implementation and use of this model, proponents have suggested several methodologies of receiving communication from God about His individual will. Of course, the actual practice of the contemporary view will vary among its advocates; however, there is general agreement on the use of the following seven methodologies of divine revelation:

- *Scripture* – While the Bible doesn't explicitly mention an individual will of God, most advocates of the contemporary view are Bible-believing Christians. Therefore, they hold that Scripture reveals God's will—in a sovereign, moral, and individual sense—and is profitable for Christian living (see 2 Tim. 3:16–17).

- *Prayer* – At Jas. 4:2, James writes, "You do not have, because you do not ask." In light of this teaching, proponents of this model often teach that prayer is a valid means of getting revelation from God about His individual will, if believers will only ask for such divine communication.

- *Personal counsel* – Within this model counsel from other believers is another means of learning God's individual will, for Solomon taught that "in abundance of counselors there is victory" (Prov. 24:6). Indeed, it is common within this model for believers to receive a word from God to share with other Christians.

- *Personal desires* – Advocates of the contemporary view teach that one's personal desires may also be a conduit for revelation of God's individual will, especially if one is walking with the Lord. David taught, "Delight yourself in the LORD, and he will give you the desires of your heart" (Ps. 37:4).

• *Circumstances* – God's providence or personal circumstances are also an important means of revelation within this model. Advocates of this approach point out that even the apostle Paul referred to open and closed doors of ministry (see 1 Cor. 16:8–9). Skill at discerning circumstances is an important part of the contemporary view.

• *Personal peace* – Likely the most often appealed to means of revelation within the contemporary view is having a personal peace about a specific choice or action. This is also referred to as the inner witness of the Holy Spirit, having a check in one's spirit, an impression, personal intuition, an unusual feeling of being led, or some similar type of concept (see John 16:13; Phil. 4:6–7; Col. 3:15).

• *Supernatural signs* – A final methodology of revelation used with the contemporary view are supernatural signs of guidance, which are analogous to those seen in Scripture. Examples would include a voice, vision, dream, angelic encounter, or some similar occurrence (see Acts 8:26; 9:3–6; 16:9–10).

According to advocates of the contemporary view, divine guidance comes when several of the above methodologies of communication from God are in one accord, with perhaps agreement between two or more of these means of revelation signaling a sure word from God.[3] Since in the application of this model agreement between any of the above methodologies is generally considered to be acceptable, these seven means of revelation are viewed as more-or-less equal—at least in practice. Surely, many who hold this approach would rightly claim the Bible to be the best form of revelation. Yet, a review of advocates' explanation of this approach reveals that in the application of this model many proponents of the contemporary view seem to place a higher emphasis on the experience of personal peace and the reception of supernatural signs of guidance. For instance, it is common for one who holds this view to justify a decision with the claim that they just "feel a peace" about a certain choice or action. Such peace is understood to be divine confirmation of a given decision.

In summary, then, there are arguments from Scripture, reason, and biblical and personal examples that have been made in favor of the contemporary view of knowing and doing the will of God. Advocates of this approach have suggested practicable guidelines by which Christians may utilize this model—that is, agreement between various forms of divine revelation. Yet, as was alluded to in the beginning of chapter 2, throughout church history this perspective on gaining divine guidance has not been the way most Christians have understood God's will to be revealed. In fact, it seems that some of the means of revelation used within the contemporary view may look quite similar to the pagan methodologies of divination discussed in the previous chapter. In light of this fact, as the contemporary view has gained popularity within the modern church, a number of critiques and limitations have been suggested by those who hold to alternative views.

Limitations of the Contemporary View

The discussion below contains a survey of challenges to the contemporary model that have been raised over time. None of these critiques are raised in malice, but rather have been suggested by some in the church who are concerned that fellow brethren may be adhering to a flawed model of knowing and doing the will of God. None of these challenges alone makes the contemporary view untenable; however, those inclined toward this model of knowing and doing God's will may wish to consider these proposed limitations as they evaluate this model in light of the ultimate arbiter of truth—that is, the Word of God.

The Concept of an Individual Will of God

One critique of the contemporary view that has been raised is the model's presupposition of and reliance upon the concept of an individual will of God, which is separate from God's sovereign will and His moral will (see the discussion in chapter 1). Throughout church history most Christians have understood the application of God's moral will in one's own life to be that which individuals are to pursue. Said differently, historically most believers have viewed the individual will of God simply to be the moral will of God applied in their own lives. This is why the church has traditionally emphasized *doing* God's will, not *discovering* God's will, for God's moral will is plainly revealed in the Bible and God clearly expects His followers to keep it (see John 14:15).

Yet, as it is commonly held, many advocates of the contemporary view teach that in order to live an optimized Christian life, characterized by happiness and personal flourishing, believers need to discover a separate individual will of God that is more specific than God's moral will. As was observed above, if one presupposes the existence of a unique individual will, then ambiguous Bible references to God's will can be cited in support of such an idea. Nevertheless, Scripture never instructs Christians to find a secret, individual will of God. Believers are, however, clearly commanded to seek God's Kingdom, which expands as Christians keep God's moral will (see Matt. 6:33). Moreover, Jesus exhorts His followers to have confidence in God's sovereign will, knowing that nothing happens apart from God's purview (see Matt. 6:31–32).

The Use of Biblical Examples

Another critique of the contemporary view relates to the model's use of biblical examples. A number of biblical examples have been offered in support of this approach, such as Abraham's servant's providential meeting of Rebecca, Ananias' being directed to visit Paul, and Philip being sent to preach to the Ethiopian eunuch. However, a closer look at these narratives reveals that they may not be as helpful as they first seem. This is so, for each of these examples was divine in orientation and extraordinary in nature.[4]

In developing a theology of God's will, we want to draw upon that which is normative in Scripture, not what is exceptional. That which makes the accounts of God directing biblical characters, like the examples cited above, so distinct is the fact that such supernatural guidance was unusual in the Bible. Viewed properly, anomalous events like those given in support of the contemporary view actually verify and affirm that which is ordinary. In other words, exceptions prove rules, not vice-versa. As such, the biblical examples cited in favor of this model should not be viewed as normative for Christian life and practice. In the Bible, when we read of miraculous instances where God directed individuals in unusual ways, we must agree that God *can* move in such ways—indeed, God can do whatever He likes. Yet, the infrequency of these occurrences should keep us from viewing and expecting these extraordinary incidents to be a regular part of the Christian life.

Unorthodox Hermeneutics

A similar critique of the contemporary view relates to advocates' use of narrative passages in the Bible to confirm the concept of an individual will of God. Most of the biblical examples used to support this view are found in the narrative passages of Scripture, such as the Old

Testament historical books or the New Testament book of Acts. Orthodox hermeneutics—that is, the science of Bible interpretation—teaches that theology ought to be constructed from the didactic (or teaching) passages of Scripture, not from unique narrative passages. Relying solely upon narrative passages to formulate one's theology can lead to what is known as the naturalistic fallacy. This fallacy entails assuming that because God *can* or *did* act in a certain manner in times past, God *does* or *will* always continue to do so in the future (see 2 Pet. 3:3–4).[5]

Orthodox hermeneutics teaches the way Christians can know how God does act, as well as how believers should respond, is to focus on what God has explicitly commanded and taught in the Bible. Of course, the narrative passages in Scripture often affirm what is taught in the didactic passages; however, when they do not (i.e., miracles or other supernatural events) the unique narrative passages should not be viewed as normative for Christian living or serve as a cornerstone in one's theology. Indeed, making narrative passages, in isolation, the fount of one's theology is dangerous, for there are many explicitly sinful narratives in Scripture.

The Use of Personal Examples

A fourth critique of the contemporary view relates to the real-life, personal examples offered in support of this model. Many of these examples may be problematic, for they are akin to self-fulfilling prophecies. To elaborate, those who accept the concept of a separate individual will of God often assume they've discovered such a will when they make a decision and life goes well for them. In contrast, when things go poorly, advocates of the contemporary model might assume they have missed God's will or have not properly understood divine guidance. So, for example, someone who takes an alternative route when driving home, on a whim, and avoids a major traffic accident might conclude they've followed God's will, while the one who is stuck in a traffic jam might believe they've somehow missed out on God's will or are perhaps being punished for some prior sin.[6]

As was discussed in the opening pages of this book, the assumption that God's will can be equated with material human flourishing is not a biblical notion; rather, it is the heresy known as the prosperity gospel. This critique may shed light on the self-focus of some who hold to the contemporary view. Indeed, it may be the case that some who seek God's individual will are using God as a means to end—that is, they are pursuing the will of God for their own well-being, not for God's glory. Yet, to make material prosperity the goal of Christianity is wrong, for the Bible teaches that it is the wicked who idolize material flourishing in this present world (see Jas. 5:1–6).[7] In contrast, Jesus taught that believers will experience various types of trials (see Matt. 10:22; John 16:33), Paul wrote that maturing Christians ought to expect persecution (see 2 Tim. 3:12), and Peter taught that God's sovereign will may be for believers to suffer and to die in service of Christ (see 1 Pet. 3:17; 4:19). Furthermore, the Bible teaches that true contentment comes when we rest in Jesus, regardless of our personal circumstances (see Phil. 4:11–12; 1 Tim. 6:6–12).

If material human flourishing is not a legitimate barometer that can be used to judge the authenticity of divine guidance, it raises the question of how advocates of the contemporary view can know they have found God's individual will. Further, even if material flourishing were a valid means of evaluating divine guidance, it seems this mechanism could only be used in retrospect. As such, the contemporary view would not be helpful for prescribing God's will in advance. Said differently, if personal flourishing was an accurate indicator of finding and following God's will, then this criteria could only be used to evaluate how we *did* live, not how we *shall* live.

The Doctrine of God

In Matt. 7:7–11 Jesus gives one of the clearest teachings in the Bible concerning God's love for mankind. Here Christ compares a human father's love for his children to that of God's love for believers. In this passage Jesus teaches, "Or which one of you, if his son asks him for bread, will give him a stone? . . . If you then, who are evil, know how to give good gifts to your children, how much more will your Father who is in heaven give good things to those who ask him!" (Matt. 7:9, 11). The idea that God the Father provides good things for His children, and that He desires an intimate relationship with believers, is reiterated all throughout Scripture. For example, at Rom. 8:32 Paul rhetorically asked the Roman Christians, "He who did not spare his own Son but gave him up for us all, how will he not also with him graciously give us all things?" Similarly, James taught the early church, "Every good gift and every perfect gift is from above, coming down from the Father" (Jas. 1:17).

A critique of the contemporary view, however, is that this model does not necessarily describe or present God as a loving Father who delights in freely giving things to His children. Rather, the contemporary view suggests that God has purposefully hidden from believers that which will bring joy to their lives—that is, the flourishing that ostensibly comes with following God's individual will. Moreover, according to the contemporary view it seems that an intimate relationship with God is not even necessary. Rather, this model teaches that in order to learn God's individual will, Christians need to develop skill at reading and utilizing various signs, many of which involve extra-biblical means of revelation. Indeed, under the contemporary model it may be possible to view God as a distant and mysterious deity, rather than the loving Father described in the Bible.

The Doctrine of Sanctification

A sixth, related critique of the contemporary view is that this approach to knowing God's will seems to circumvent the process of sanctification. To elaborate, historically the church has held that as believers are sanctified—that is, as they grow in their understanding of Scripture and cultivate their relationship with God—they will gain knowledge of God's moral will and will grow in their desire and ability to conform to such standards. Yet, by sometimes focusing on extra-biblical revelation, the contemporary view unintentionally marginalizes the need for believers to cultivate an ever-maturing relationship with God. This is so, for this model often emphasizes proficiency at receiving extra-biblical revelation, not growth in one's relationship with God. While there may be a veneer of spirituality to the idea of receiving extra-biblical revelation, ironically, immaturity is actually fostered when sanctification is reduced to following a divine script. So, although it may seem more exciting to pursue extra-biblical revelation than to cultivate knowledge of the Bible, such a pursuit doesn't require (and may even discourage) the process of sanctification.

The Doctrine of Scripture

A seventh critique of the contemporary view relates to the doctrine of Scripture. A cornerstone doctrine of the sixteenth century Protestant Reformation is the doctrine of *sola Scriptura*, which teaches that Scripture alone is authoritative for Christian faith and practice. This doctrine arises out of passages such as 2 Tim. 3:16, where Paul wrote, "Scripture is breathed out by God and profitable for teaching, for reproof, for correction, and for training in righteousness." This same idea can be seen at 2 Pet. 1:3 where, in reference to Scripture, Peter taught that God's "divine power has granted to us all things that pertain to life and godliness" (see 2 Pet. 1:19–21). In light of passages such as these, Protestant believers have traditionally affirmed the doctrine of *sola Scriptura*, as well as the related concepts of the inerrancy, infallibility, and sufficiency of the Bible (see John 10:35).

A critique raised against the contemporary view is that in looking to extra-biblical revelation as a means of discerning God's individual will, this model may functionally deny the doctrine of *sola Scriptura*. As has been noted, since the Bible does not explicitly mention an individual will of God that is separate from God's moral will, advocates of the contemporary view often utilize extra-biblical methodologies in order to receive divine guidance. Yet, in so doing, they essentially and practically deny this cornerstone Protestant doctrine, for if Scripture is authoritative for Christian faith and practice, there is no need to look elsewhere. Said differently, if the will of God has already been revealed in the Bible, and Scripture is sufficient for Christian living, then decision-making ought not to emphasize the reception of extra-biblical revelation; rather, the focus of believers' lives should be upon obedience to that which has already been revealed in the Bible.

Impractical Application

A final critique of the contemporary view relates to the application of this model. It seems that proponents of this view are inconsistent in the methodologies they use to receive extra-biblical guidance, as well as in the types of decisions for which this model is employed. For instance, it is common for those who hold to the contemporary view to metaphorically "put out a fleece" in seeking divine guidance. For example, concerning future employment, one could propose a scenario in which a job offer within a certain salary range would be understood to be a sign from God.[8] Yet, proponents of this view would likely scoff at the idea of receiving verbal career guidance from one's dog or cat. However, both Gideon's fleece and Balaam's donkey were one-time events, recorded within the narrative passages of Scripture, where God's will was disclosed. There does not seem to be a good reason to favor one of these narratives over the other.

Advocates of the contemporary view are also inconsistent in applying this model only in "important" decisions, such as career choices, marriage and family issues, and major financial purchases. The problem is that this view has no inherent way to determine which decisions really are "important." Since Scripture is silent on the individual will of God, as well as on the utilization of this view, in order to be consistent, it would seem this model ought to be used for every decision in life, ranging from the important to the mundane. After all, the smallest life decision, such as which shirt to wear to a job interview, could have a great impact on the "important" issues of life. Of course, it would be quite laborious—if not entirely impossible—to try and discern God's individual will for every choice in life. However, within the contemporary view, the alternative is to make artificial distinctions about the "important" decisions of life.

Conclusion

While all readers may not be familiar with the phrase "contemporary view," the system described in this chapter is likely familiar to many churchgoers today. By default, in the modern context, many Christians assume there is an individual will of God they must discover and pursue in order to have a fulfilled life. Indeed, fear of missing God's will is a cause of anxiety among many modern believers. Yet, as this chapter has demonstrated, the contemporary view is not without a number of challenges and limitations. Although the critiques of this model given in this chapter do not make the contemporary view untenable, they may leave readers wondering if there is another, better approach to knowing and doing God's will. In the next chapter we'll turn our attention to an alternative model of divine guidance—that is, the traditional view.

Summary Points

• The contemporary view can be argued by appealing to Bible verses, reason, as well as personal and scriptural examples. In explaining this view, personal and biblical examples are likely the most common defense.

• Advocates of the contemporary view seek guidance from God by appealing to agreement among several forms of revelation, which include Scripture, prayer, personal counsel, personal desires, circumstances, personal peace, and supernatural signs.

• The most frequently appealed to means of extra-biblical revelation among advocates of the contemporary model are personal peace and supernatural signs. Within the practice of this view, these means are sometimes appealed to more often than Scripture.

• One of the most significant critiques of the contemporary view is its assertion that there is an individual will of God that must be discovered by Christians. This is problematic, for Scripture does not explicitly identify a separate individual will of God.

• Major theological critiques of the contemporary view include this model's doctrine of God, doctrine of sanctification, and doctrine of Scripture. These challenges, coupled with the model's hermeneutic, may leave some looking for an alternative approach.

David W. Jones

CHAPTER 4:
THE TRADITIONAL VIEW

Throughout history, the way most Christians have sought divine guidance and gained knowledge of God's will is through reading the Bible. One of the most well-known teaching tools in the Protestant tradition is *The Westminster Shorter Catechism*, which was written in 1646–47. Question two of this historical catechism asks, "What rule hath God given to direct us how we may glorify and enjoy Him?" The supplied answer in the catechism is, "The Word of God, which is contained in the Scriptures of the Old and New Testaments, is the *only* rule to direct us how we may glorify and enjoy Him." Throughout history the idea that the Bible is "the only rule to direct us," which is very similar to the concept of *sola Scriptura* discussed in chapter 3, has been the prevailing view among Protestants. In fact, the teaching that Scripture is the way in which God guides His people has been so common throughout history that this idea can be called the traditional view.[1] We'll explore and explain this approach to knowing God's will in this chapter.

In short, the traditional view holds that there are only two wills of God: the moral will of God, which is revealed in the moral precepts of Scripture, and the sovereign will of God, which is unknowable prior to its manifestation.[2] Advocates of the traditional view do not endorse the concept of a separate individual will of God in the same sense as do those who champion the contemporary view. Yet, within this model the basic concept of an individual will of God is still relevant, for personal guidance can be understood to be the moral will of God manifest in the life of an individual believer. In light of these dynamics, proponents of the traditional view do not focus on discovering a separate, secret individual will of God via extra-biblical means of revelation; rather, they focus on knowing the contents of the Bible and applying the moral precepts of Scripture to everyday life.[3]

Given its denial of a separate individual will of God, at first glance the traditional view may seem to portray God as being cold and distant from mankind. Yet, those who hold this model claim just the opposite is true. To elaborate, the traditional view teaches the very goal of the Christian life is to cultivate an intimate relationship with God, through knowledge of His Word, so that believers will be equipped to understand and to keep God's moral will. Said differently, the objective of the traditional view is to develop the mind of Christ, which is revealed in Scripture,[4] so that believers are able to think God's thoughts after Him and to act in a Christ-like manner in every circumstance of life. In contrast, as was noted in the previous chapter, the contemporary view does not emphasize (nor does it preclude) growth and intimacy in one's relationship with God; rather, in practice, it focuses on developing skill at receiving extra-biblical revelation. Ironically, then, it is the contemporary view that allows for a distant relationship with God, while the traditional view necessitates divine intimacy.

Wisdom and the Traditional View

A major emphasis within the traditional view is the

attainment of divine wisdom. Scripture exhorts believers to ask for wisdom from God. For example, James writes, "If any of you lacks wisdom, let him ask God, who gives generously to all without reproach, and it will be given him" (Jas. 1:5; see Prov. 2:1–5; 4:4–7). Solomon teaches that wisdom starts with the fear or reverence of God that stems from one's relationship with the Lord (see Prov. 1:7; 9:10). The beginning of wisdom, then, is the ability to evaluate life in light of one's kinship with and knowledge of God. In other words, wisdom is the ability to see life from God's perspective and to act accordingly. Since we gain knowledge of God through the Bible, wisdom can be defined as the skill of practically applying God's Word to daily living. Wisdom makes the connection between God's moral will and real life. The more intimate is our relationship with God, the more wisdom we will have attained; thus, the more moral our thoughts and actions will be (see Eph. 5:15–17; Heb. 5:12–14).

The traditional view holds that the normative pattern of Christian living is to make decisions that are reflective of one's walk with Christ and are in accord with the moral precepts revealed in Scripture.[5] Since "all the treasures of wisdom and knowledge" (Col. 2:3) are hidden in Christ, more often than not, decisions made by maturing Christians will be wise decisions that manifest God's moral will (see Col. 1:9–10). Furthermore, such wise decisions will result in human flourishing, as is defined by God,[6] for Jesus taught His followers that "wisdom is justified by her deeds" (Matt. 11:19). According to its advocates, then, the traditional view is the key to pleasing God, to experiencing personal fulfillment, to displaying the gospel, and to furthering God's Kingdom. Since the moral will of God, which is revealed in the Bible, is so foundational to the traditional view, this concept warrants further investigation.

The Moral Will of God

God's moral will is most clearly communicated through His moral laws and commands revealed in the Bible. It is easy to misunderstand God's moral laws, viewing them as autocratic precepts designed to stifle human freedom. Indeed, given our sin nature, such a legalistic conception of God's moral laws is understandable; yet, it is incorrect. Rather than describing the moral law in burdensome terms, the Bible teaches that God's moral commands are "holy and righteous" (Rom. 7:12). In fact, Paul taught the Corinthian church that "keeping the commandments of God is what matters" (1 Cor. 7:19, NKJV). Later, Paul exhorted Timothy toward Christian living, writing that "the law is good" (1 Tim. 1:8). James, the half-brother of Jesus, even refers to the moral law twice in his epistle as the perfect "law of liberty" (Jas. 1:25; 2:12). In James' estimation, then, the moral law ought not to be viewed as a legalistic burden, but as a life-giving blessing.[7]

As I have explained elsewhere,[8] God's moral laws can be understood as a revelation of God's own moral character and will. For instance, the sixth commandment says, "You shall not murder" (Exod. 20:13). This negative command could be stated positively as, "You shall respect innocent human life." Whether stated positively or negatively, though, this moral law was not arbitrarily given by God. Rather, this law about respecting human life is part of God's revelation of His own character and will, for God Himself is the source and the sustainer of all human life (see John 11:25; 14:6). Therefore, in commanding His followers to not murder, God is exhorting believers to become like Him—that is, to act like Him and to functionally bear God's image (see Matt. 5:48). When Christians keep the sixth commandment, then, they embody God's moral will, become Christ-like, and reflect God's character before a watching world. In other words, when believers obey God's moral precepts they keep His moral will and are sanctified. This same dynamic is true for each part of God's moral law that is given to man.

Of course, it is possible to disobey God's moral laws and thus to reject God's moral will. When this happens, God's will is not done, which is the very antithesis of the Lord's Prayer (see Matt. 6:10). To illustrate, since God is always faithful to those with whom He has an intimate relationship (see Deut. 31:6; Matt. 28:20), God has commanded His image-bearers to act likewise. This aspect of God's moral will is summarized, albeit in a marital context, in the seventh commandment, which reads, "You shall not commit adultery" (Exod. 20:14). When Judas betrayed Christ for thirty pieces of silver, he chose to do his own will, rather than God's moral will, and thus was not faithful in his relationship with Jesus. In so doing, Judas violated the moral law and acted in a profoundly un-Christ-like manner. Since man was created to do God's will and to bear God's image, Judas' betrayal of Jesus was also a profoundly un-human act. Both Matthew and Luke report that this resulted in Judas' eventually taking his own life, for the end result of mankind rejecting the moral will of God is always despair (Matt. 27:3–8; Acts 1:16–19). We must remember that God creates us to do what He tells us to do.

God's moral will is also revealed in the person of Jesus Christ. As the writer of Hebrews explains, "Long ago, at many times and in many ways, God spoke to our fathers by the prophets, but in these last days he has spoken to us by his Son" (Heb. 1:1–2). Since the record of Jesus' life and teaching is contained in the Gospels, this is yet another way in which Scripture becomes a rule to direct us in Christian living. So, in addition to reading the moral precepts of Scripture, we can know God's will by looking at the example of Jesus as recorded in the Gospel narratives. Observe, however, that this is really one means of revelation, for the moral law is a revelation of God's moral will, and Jesus is God.[9] The narrative of Christ's ministry, then, is a record of Jesus keeping the moral law. Thus, Christ could testify, "Do not think that I have come to abolish the Law or the Prophets; I have not come to abolish them but to fulfill them" (Matt. 5:17). Indeed, being fully God, the man Jesus Christ could not do otherwise.[10]

Another, less precise, way in which God's moral will is revealed is through general revelation. General revelation can be defined as God's revelation of Himself to all peoples, at all times, in all places. While an in-depth discussion of this topic is beyond the scope of this book,[11] we can observe the Bible's teaching that God has revealed His moral standards to mankind, in a general way, via the created order (see Ps. 19:1–4; Rom. 1:18–20), the human conscience (see Rom. 2:14–15), and the record of history (see Acts 14:17; 17:24–27). Although advocates of the traditional view would not support using any of these means of revelation in isolation, general revelation can be used in conjunction with Scripture in order to confirm God's moral laws and thus His moral will. For example, Scripture explicitly records that it is God's moral will for mankind to labor in order to meet his own material needs (see Exod. 20:15; Eph. 4:28). General revelation confirms this truth, as those who do not labor are often plagued with a guilty conscience, fall into poverty, and develop an unbiblical sense of entitlement.[12] Conversely, those who do labor generally experience contentment, a sense of accomplishment, and have their material needs met.

In sum, then, the traditional view is based upon the idea that God has comprehensively revealed His moral will to mankind in the Bible. This is seen primarily in the moral precepts of Scripture and in the example of Jesus, as well as being reflected in general revelation. Proponents of the traditional view assert that the revelation of God's moral will in the Bible is sufficient for Christian life and practice; thus, there is no need to look to extra-biblical revelation for divine guidance. Advocates of the traditional view admit that God is free to supernaturally guide people apart from Scripture—as God is free to perform any miracle—however, believers ought not to expect such events to be a normative part of the Christian life. As we further investigate knowing and doing God's will, in the following section we'll look at a complement to God's moral will within the traditional view—that is, God's sovereign will.

The Sovereign Will of God

Knowledge of the moral will of God is an essential component of the traditional view. However, as believers pursue God's moral will and experience the blessings and trials of life, an understanding of the sovereign will of God is also important. God has always had a master plan that includes His dealings with mankind and His governance of the world. Even the death of Jesus, writes Luke, happened "according to the definite plan and foreknowledge of God" (Acts 2:23; see Gal. 4:4–5). This unfolding of God's master plan for the world constitutes God's sovereign will. God's sovereign will, then, entails everything that God has eternally decreed and it includes everything that comes to pass.[13] As was noted in chapter 1 of this book, this is the concept that is usually in view when Scripture mentions the will of God. Thus, while the sovereign will of God may be a challenging topic to wrap one's mind around, it is a prevalent and recurring theme throughout the Bible.

God's sovereign will is based upon God's own desires and eternal purposes. In regard to the sovereign will of God, Job observed, "What he desires, that he does" (Job 23:13; see Ps. 115:3). Similarly, Isaiah writes about God's sovereign will as he records God's declaration, "I am God, and there is no other; I am God, and there is none like me, declaring the end from the beginning and from ancient times things not yet done, saying, 'My counsel shall stand, and I will accomplish all my purpose,' . . . . I have spoken, and I will bring it to pass; I have purposed, and I will do it" (Isa. 46:9–11). Even King Nebuchadnezzar, who was at one time the most powerful monarch in the world, concluded that God "does according to his will among the host of heaven and among the inhabitants of the earth; and none can stay his hand or say to him, 'What have you done?'" (Dan. 4:35). God's sovereign will, then, is contingent upon nothing apart from Him and always comes to pass.

The sovereign will of God cannot be known in advance (outside of prophecy) and it cannot be avoided once manifest. Concerning God's sovereign will, Moses wrote, "The secret things belong to the LORD our God" (Deut. 29:29; see Rom. 11:33–36). Given that God's sovereign will is unknowable prior to it being revealed, it is not something that one can find or even choose to obey. Rather, it is an ever-present reality that is unfolded moment by moment. The concept of God's sovereign will can help mankind to properly view the blessings and trials of life, as well as to affirm the goodness of God, regardless of one's experience in a particular moment. Unlike God's moral will, which can be followed or ignored, God's sovereign will is inviolable—that is, it is impossible to be outside of the sovereign will of God. God's sovereign will, then, ought not to be feared, for it is a concept from which believers can draw comfort, knowing that nothing happens apart from God's purview and purposes (see Matt. 10:29–31).

Since God's sovereign will entails everything that comes to pass, it is not dependent upon mankind for its actualization. In other words, God's sovereign will is not impacted by man's obedience or disobedience to His moral will. Indeed, God is able even to use man's sin for His own sovereign purposes. For example, King David committed adultery with Bathsheba, which included the murder of her husband Uriah; yet, in time, God used this union to produce Solomon, the wisest person ever to live (see 2 Samuel 11–12). Similarly, God used Joseph's brothers' sins of jealously, lying, and the selling of their own sibling into slavery in order to save all Israel from a great famine (see Gen. 45:5–8; 50:19–20). Perhaps the greatest example of God using man's sin to accomplish His sovereign will is the crucifixion of Jesus. At Acts 3:13–21 Peter taught that although this event was done freely by the Jewish leaders and Roman authorities, it was also the fulfillment of prophecy and made possible a way for all men to be reconciled to God.

The Doctrine of Providence

The manifestation of God's sovereign will in the world is commonly referred to as the doctrine of providence. One way in which the traditional view differs from the contemporary view is in how the doctrine of providence is understood. To elaborate, many who hold to the contemporary view believe it is possible to "read" providence. This practice entails trying to discern the way in which God is moving within one's own life, and in the broader world, and thereby to reach conclusions about God's individual will. A common exhortation in this vein of thought is, to find out where God is working in the world and to join Him. Among advocates of the contemporary view this process of extrapolating the individual will of God from the sovereign will of God is commonly referred to as "looking for open or closed doors."

In contrast to the contemporary view, advocates of the traditional view note that believers are never commanded in the Bible to attempt to "read" providence (see Eccl. 3:11); rather, they are commanded to keep God's moral law.[14] This is why David refused to kill King Saul, on two separate occasions, despite the seemingly favorable circumstances and the imminent danger to his own life (see 1 Sam. 24:4–7; 26:1–25). On these two instances David chose to trust in God and to keep God's moral law prohibiting murder, rather than viewing the opportunity to kill Saul as a providential revelation of God's individual will. Moreover, in both of these narratives David rebuked those who suggested that he slay the king, even referring to Saul numerous times as "the LORD's anointed" (1 Sam. 24:6, 10; 26:9, 11, 16, 23).[15] Of course, since David loved the law, he knew that Deut. 13:1–3 taught God's people that signs, wonders, and otherwise favorable circumstances are not proof of divine leading.[16] Indeed, providences are not self-interpreting, but must be viewed through the lens of God's Word, which includes His moral commands.

The example of Paul is also instructive in regard to the doctrine of providence. In writing to the church at Corinth, Paul justified his extended stay in Ephesus by noting that "a wide door for effective work has opened to me" (1 Cor. 16:9). While we may be tempted to use Paul's account here to justify attempts at reading providence, we must observe his later statement to these same Corinthian believers, "When I came to Troas to preach the gospel of Christ, *even though a door* was *opened for me in the Lord*, my spirit was not at rest because I did not find my brother Titus there. So I took leave of them and went on to Macedonia" (2 Cor. 2:12–13). So, by his own testimony, Paul did not walk through a door of ministry in Troas that had been opened for him by the Lord. It seems clear, then, that in Pauline terminology "open doors" and "closed doors" are not manifestations of divine guidance; rather, they are just opportunities for Christian service that fall within the sovereign will of God (see Col. 4:2–3).[17]

Analysis of Key Passages

In seeking to better understand the traditional view, it may be helpful to see how those who hold this approach to knowing God's will interpret key passages in the Bible that have been used to support the idea of a separate, hidden, individual will of God. In this section we'll briefly look at three Scripture passages often cited by proponents of the contemporary view and see how these passages are interpreted within the traditional view. The passages we'll survey are Ps. 32:8; Prov. 3:5–6; and Rom. 12:2.

The theme of Psalm 32, which is one of seven penitential psalms in the Bible,[18] is the joy of divine forgiveness. Traditionally, the church has understood this psalm to record David's reflections about God's forgiveness upon his confession of adultery with Bathsheba (see Psalm 51). After writing about his sin and repentance in Ps. 32:1–7, at Ps. 32:8 David reports God's response to him, "I will instruct you and teach you in the way you should go; I will counsel you with my eye upon you." Some view this verse to be a timeless, divine promise to disclose a secret, individual will of God to believers. Advocates of the traditional view, however, assert that when read in context, this verse is better understood to be a summary of God's rebuke of David, through the prophet Nathan, which included the prospect of God continuing to instruct David through the Word of God (see 2 Sam. 12:13; Ps. 51:12–13). Such an interpretation seems more logical than viewing Ps. 32:8 to be an isolated verse about God's individual will in the midst of David's reflections about forgiveness for transgressing God's moral will.

Another passage often cited in support of an individual will of God is Prov. 3:5–6. These well-known verses read, "Trust in the Lord with all your heart, and lean not on your own understanding; in all your ways acknowledge Him, and He shall direct your paths" (NKJV). It is easy to see how this passage could be used to support the contemporary view—especially if the presupposition of an individual will of God is brought to the text. However, traditional view advocates note that when the term "paths" is used in the Psalms and Proverbs it always denotes the general course of life, not an individual will of God.[19] Moreover, the verb "direct," when used in conjunction with the term "paths," carries the idea of making smooth, not the provision of personal, divine guidance. This is why many modern translations render the last phrase in this passage, "He will make your ways straight," or a similar translation. Furthermore, understanding Prov. 3:5–6 to be a general promise of divine blessing, rather than a specific promise of extra-biblical guidance, is in accord with a recurring theme in the book of Proverbs—that is, the contrast between the fool, who follows his own will to ruin, and the wise man, who follows God's moral will to flourishing (see Prov. 4:18–19; 11:5; 15:19).

A final verse that has been used to justify the idea of an individual will of God is Rom. 12:2. In this passage Paul exhorts his readers, "And do not be conformed to this world, but be transformed by the renewing of your mind, that you may prove what is that good and acceptable and perfect will of God" (NKJV). Proponents of the traditional view hold that this verse is not prescribing a way by which believers can know a secret, individual will of God. Rather, this passage is encouraging Christians to learn the moral truths that had been taught in Romans 1–11, for doing so would demonstrate the goodness of God's commands. The word "prove" in this verse means to demonstrate or to authenticate, which explains why the term is translated as "test" in many modern translations. Furthermore, in this verse Paul is juxtaposing worldly values with godly values. Given this context, it seems more logical to understand Paul's citation of the "will of God" in this passage to be a reference to God's moral will, not an appeal to a secret individual will of God.[20]

As the above brief analysis of three proof-texts for the contemporary view has shown, it is not necessary to interpret ambiguous citations of God's will in the Bible to be references to a secret, individual will of God. While such passages could be references to a hidden will of God, the deciding factor in interpreting such passages must be the context—including the immediate verses in which the references occur and the larger, systematic, biblical teaching on the will of God.

Implementing the Traditional View

Having studied the nuances of the traditional view, including its relationship to biblical wisdom, the place of God's moral and sovereign wills within this approach, and the way in which advocates of this model interpret key Scripture passages related to God's will, we are now ready to look at how this view can be utilized in the process of making decisions and doing the will of God. In the discussion that follows we'll cover five suggestions or steps that can be taken in order to implement the traditional view. Note that we'll give an example of the utilization of these steps in chapter 6 of this book.

First, and most importantly, we must remember that God's moral will is comprehensively revealed in the Bible, especially in God's moral law. In writing about God's revelation, Peter taught, "His divine power has granted to us all things that pertain to life and godliness" (2 Pet. 1:3). Indeed, there is no area of life in which moral decisions can be made, which is not addressed by God's Word. Of course, the areas of life in which Scripture applies are endless—and change with time, culture, and technology—yet, the underlying moral law, which reveals God's moral will, is comprehensive and unchanging. Cultivating an understanding of the Bible, then, is essential in knowing and doing God's will. Such knowledge must be gained over time through Bible reading, Bible study, memorizing Scripture, participating in local church life, and receiving biblical counsel from mature Christians, such as one's pastor[21]—among other ways in which we may learn the contents of God's Word.

Second, in seeking to know and to do God's will, we must pray. As was noted earlier in this chapter, James instructs his readers to pray for wisdom as he writes, "If any of you lacks wisdom, let him ask God, who gives generously to all without reproach, and it will be given him" (Jas. 1:5). Believers can also pray for self-understanding. This is important, for oftentimes God's will is obscured to us because we are blinded by our own will, our lack of knowledge, and our selfish ambitions. Indeed, a complaint about not knowing God's will is often a confession about not knowing God's Word. David modeled a prayer for self-understanding in Psalm 139, where he asked, "Search me, O God, and know my heart! Try me and know my thoughts! And see if there be any grievous way in me, and lead me in the way everlasting!" (Ps. 139:23–24). Christians can also pray for discernment regarding opportunities in life, relationships with others, and in any situation in which wisdom is needed (see Phil. 1:9–11). However, we must keep in mind that prayer is about *sanctification* not extra-biblical *revelation*. We'll look at the doctrine of prayer in more depth in the following chapter.

Third, in pursuing the will of God we can consider our own gifts, abilities, opportunities, and even personal desires. Spiritual gifts, which often are used in conjunction with one's natural abilities, are given for the edification of the Body of Christ (see 1 Cor. 12:7; 14:12). Since God's will is the sanctification of the church (see 1 Thess. 4:3), the best course of action for an individual believer is always the one that is most spiritually expedient—that is, the path that best furthers the Kingdom of God. Along these lines, in Ps. 37:4, David taught, "Delight yourself in the LORD, and he will give you the desires of your heart." Here David is not describing God as a magic genie who grants the wishes of believers; rather, David is teaching that as we gain knowledge of God through His Word, God changes the very desires of our hearts. Through sanctification God's thoughts become our thoughts, God's purposes become our purposes, and God's will becomes our will. The more like Christ we become, the more focused we are at building God's Kingdom, and the less concerned we are with building our own kingdom.

Fourth, as we deliberate about God's will, we must consider the example of, and receive counsel from, the people of God in Scripture, in history, and in contemporary life. The author of the book of Hebrews instructed the church, "Remember your leaders, those who spoke to you the word of God. Consider the outcome of their way of life, and imitate their faith" (Heb. 13:7). This exhortation was relevant in biblical times and it applies in the contemporary setting too. Whatever challenges and topics arise in life, it is important for believers to remember that others have labored over similar types of issues. Their example and instructions are beneficial for others wrestling with the same kinds of questions. Likewise, we must remember that we serve as examples to others. Paul was cognizant of this fact, as he urged his readers on at least five different occasions, "Be imitators of me" (1 Cor. 4:16; 11:1; Phil. 3:17; 4:9; 2 Thess. 3:7).

Fifth, and finally, as we engage in God's will we must evaluate the potential effects of our decisions upon ourselves and upon others. As we'll discuss in the following chapter, in regard to some issues there is a degree of personal freedom within God's will. This is not to say that God's moral will is ever subjective or changing; rather, the application of God's will may be affected in a given situation by factors such as one's conscience and the presence of weaker brethren. In light of these dynamics, Paul wrote to the Corinthian church and declared, "All things are lawful for me, but not all things are helpful; all things are lawful for me, but I will not be dominated by anything" (1 Cor. 6:12). In other words, Paul taught that just because an act is permissible within God's moral will does not mean that it is always the best course of action. Similarly, at 1 Cor. 10:23, Paul wrote, "All things are lawful, but not all things are helpful; all things are lawful, but not all things build up." Here Paul taught that our actions should not hurt the Body of Christ; rather, they should build it up. Indeed, this is the spirit of Christian liberty (see Rom. 14:14, 23; 1 Cor. 7:27–31; Gal. 5:13; 1 Tim. 4:4). We'll return to this subject in the following chapter.

In summary, then, in utilizing the traditional view we can consider five Bible-centered suggestions: (1) focus upon the content of Scripture; (2) pray for wisdom, self-understanding, and discernment; (3) consider our own gifts, abilities, opportunities, and desires; (4) look to the example of and counsel from other mature believers; and (5) evaluate the potential effects of our decisions upon others. If these steps or suggestions are implemented, believers will be in a position to follow God's revealed will and confidently make decisions that will glorify God.

Conclusion

As this chapter has demonstrated, the traditional view of knowing and doing the will of God stands in contrast to the contemporary view. Whereas, in its usual manifestation, the contemporary view focuses upon developing skill at receiving extra-biblical guidance in order to find an individual will of God, the traditional view focuses on fostering one's relationship with God by growing in knowledge of the Bible. For traditional view advocates, understanding God's revealed moral will in Scripture, and applying it to one's life, is the key to spiritual growth and flourishing in the Christian life. In the next chapter we'll turn our attention to three issues that relate to the traditional view—that is, the place of prayer in moral decision making, the role of the Holy Spirit in following God's will, and navigating God's will in regard to Christian liberty.

Summary Points

• The traditional view does not focus on discovering a separate, secret individual will of God via extra-biblical means of revelation; rather, it focuses on knowing the contents of the Bible and applying the moral precepts of Scripture to everyday life.

• Within the traditional view, the individual will of God can be thought of as the moral will of God, which is comprehensively revealed within the Bible, applied in a particular individual's life.

• Biblical wisdom, which can be defined as the skill of practically applying God's Word to daily living, is a key component of the traditional view, for wisdom makes the connection between God's moral will and real life.

• Advocates of the traditional view hold that there are two separate wills of God: the moral will of God and the sovereign will of God. God's moral will includes all of God's commands in Scripture, and God's sovereign will entails everything that comes to pass.

• The actualization of God's sovereign will is referred to as the doctrine of providence. Proponents of the traditional view hold that it is impossible, unnecessary, and unbiblical to attempt to read providence.

CHAPTER 5:
PRAYER, THE HOLY SPIRIT, AND CHRISTIAN LIBERTY

Within the traditional view, the pursuit of God's will can spark questions about related issues. As the previous chapter explained, the core of the traditional view is the claim that the Bible alone is sufficient for Christian life and practice. Scripture comprehensively reveals God's moral will, and obedience to the moral will of God is what individual believers are to pursue. While there is certainly a degree of freedom in the application of God's moral will, the traditional view asserts there is no decision one could face in life that is not covered by the moral will of God, which is revealed in the Bible. This teaching is fairly straightforward; however, questions sometimes arise about tangential issues, such as: how prayer relates to the will of God, the role of the Holy Spirit in making moral decisions, and the place of Christian liberty in knowing God's will. The aim of this chapter is to explore these three related topics and to show how they are understood within the traditional view.

Prayer and the Will of God

As we've surveyed the contemporary and traditional views over the previous two chapters, we noted that the practice of prayer is appealed to by advocates of both of these models. Certainly, as we ponder the will of God, prayer is an important discipline, for Jesus taught His followers to pray to God about His will, saying, "Your kingdom come, *your will be done*, on earth as it is in heaven" (Matt. 6:10). Moreover, by way of example, the Gospels report that many of the decisions and events in Christ's life were preceded by a season of prayer (see Luke 5:16; 6:12) and, on more than one occasion, Jesus explicitly taught His followers about prayer (see Matt. 6:5–15; Luke 11:1–4). In order to follow Christ's example and instructions, then, believers must pray as they seek to implement God's will in their lives. Indeed, prayer is an indispensable Christian discipline. Note that James taught the church, in a well-known verse, "The prayer of a righteous person has great power" (Jas. 5:16).[1]

While advocates of both the contemporary and traditional views rightly appeal to prayer, they differ in how they conceive of the practice. To elaborate, many advocates of the contemporary view understand prayer to be a means by which believers can gain specific, extra-biblical guidance from God. Within the contemporary view such revelation may take the form of a feeling of personal peace while praying, or be tied to a supernatural sign, such as a voice, vision, impression, or unusual sense of being led. Within the traditional view, however, prayer is not understood to be a normative means of revelation; rather, it is viewed primarily as a means of sanctification. Proponents of the traditional view assert that God speaks to believers through the Bible, and that believers can speak to God—that is, answer God and respond to His revelation in Scripture—through prayer. Said differently, within the traditional view prayer entails *communing* with

God around His Word, not getting extra-biblical *communication* from God.[2]

Advocates of the traditional view teach that prayer is an expression before God of one's faith, trust, and love for God and His people. It is made possible through the mediation of Christ (see 1 Tim. 2:5), is rooted in one's relationship with Jesus, and can concern any issues or questions that arise over the course of one's life. Indeed, within the Bible, believers are invited to cast all of their cares upon Christ (see 1 Pet. 5:7). Just as we share our concerns and burdens with those whom we love, so we ought to intimately commune with Jesus about the trials and triumphs of our lives. Although traditional view advocates do not look for extra-biblical revelation through prayer, there is a tangible sweetness of fellowship that comes with being in Christ's presence and meditating upon His Word, which is illuminated by the Holy Spirit. Such fellowship in prayer, accompanied by personal reflection, can lead to a deeper knowledge of Scripture, the eyes of one's heart being enlightened (see Eph. 1:18), greater confidence in God's Word, as well as a better overall understanding of how biblical truth applies to one's life.

Prayer and God's Moral Will

Within the traditional view, prayer is not regarded as a means to get God to do our will, but as a way to properly orient us toward His moral will. As we mature via exposure to Scripture, the discipline of prayer creates within ourselves a right perspective on God's will. Further, the more of God's moral will we know in Scripture, the better our prayers will become. John wrote, "Whatever we ask we receive from him, because we keep his commandments and do what pleases him" (1 John 3:22). In this passage, John is not teaching that law-keeping somehow indebts God to answer our prayers. Rather, he is reminding believers that our knowledge of and obedience to God's moral law will inform our prayers. As we mature spiritually our prayers become less self-focused and more in accord with God's moral will.[3] Prayer, then, is not an attempt to get new information from God; rather, it arises out of exposure to God's moral law in the Bible, which gives us revelation about ourselves and, in turn, shapes our prayers.

Of course, our prayers are not always answered in the way in which we desire, but God always gives us what we need.[4] Sometimes the reason why our prayers are not answered as we'd like is because our prayers are self-focused, arising out of our own will, not God's moral will. James wrote, "You ask and do not receive, because you ask wrongly, to spend it on your passions" (Jas. 4:3). Conversely, when our prayers are properly oriented and rooted in God's revealed will, they are answered as we desire, for as we draw near to Christ, His desires become our desires (see Ps. 37:4).[5] Jesus taught His disciples, "I say to you, whatever you ask of the Father in my name, he will give it to you" (John 16:23). To pray in Jesus' name, then, is to pray in accord with Christ's character and moral will.[6] It is to pray as Jesus would pray.

Sometimes we do not know what or how to pray, for we are unsure of how God's moral will relates to or can be applied in our present situation. On such occasions, we can be comforted in knowing that God is always aware of our needs, even before we ask Him (see Matt. 6:8), and He knows our thoughts, even before we articulate them (see Ps. 139:4). Moreover, Paul taught that the "Spirit intercedes for the saints according to the will of God" (Rom. 8:27), and the writer of Hebrews wrote that Christ "is able to save to the uttermost those who draw near to God through him, since he always lives to make intercession for them" (Heb. 7:25). So, even in times when we are spiritually weak or confused about how to pray, we can rest assured that God is continually working on our behalf and for His own glory.

Prayer and God's Sovereign Will

Prayer, then, is intimately tied to God's moral will as revealed in the Bible. An important issue, however, is the relationship between prayer and God's sovereign will. In the first chapter of this book we noted that God's sovereign will refers to everything that God has eternally decreed, and it includes everything that comes to pass. Given the comprehensive nature of God's sovereign will, some may conclude that prayer is unnecessary. Yet, while God's sovereign will is all-encompassing, Scripture teaches that prayer has great value, for it is part of God's master plan for the world. In the Bible we learn that God has incorporated prayer into His sovereign will. Indeed, God has determined that His master plan for the world will be unfolded by and fulfilled through the prayers of His saints. In other words, God has decreed both the ends and the means for accomplishing His will. Prayer, then, does not change what God has purposed to do; rather, it is the means by which He achieves His sovereign will.

A good example of the relationship between prayer and God's sovereign will is the salvation of mankind. Scripture declares that "salvation belongs to the Lord" (Jonah 2:9), and Jesus taught, "No one can come to me unless the Father who sent me draws him" (John 6:44). Clearly, then, salvation is of God and is part of His sovereign will. Moreover, Paul teaches that even the expressed faith by which mankind is saved is a gift from God (see Eph. 2:8–9). Yet, the Bible repeatedly exhorts believers to pray for the lost (see Acts 26:18; Rom. 10:1; 1 Tim. 2:1–6). Furthermore, God has chosen to birth faith in the hearts of mankind by the hearing of the Word of God, which is preached by man (see Matt. 28:18–20; Rom. 10:17). As we obediently pray for the lost and indiscriminately share the gospel with all men, God is pleased to unfold His plan of redemption. So, as is illustrated by the process of salvation, the free prayers and actions of mankind are an indispensable part of the unfolding of God's sovereign will.

It is clear, then, that prayer is not contrary to or rendered impotent by God's sovereign will. Prayer is part of God's sovereign will. This is why Paul taught the believers at Corinth, "We are God's fellow workers" (1 Cor. 3:9) and could later write, "[We are] working together with him" (2 Cor. 6:1). In conceiving of the relationship between God's moral will, God's sovereign will, and prayer, we can conclude that prayer is prescribed within God's moral will and is incorporated within God's sovereign will. Through prayer believers are kept focused upon God's moral will and become God's fellow laborers in accomplishing His sovereign will. There is no conflict between prayer and the will of God.

In summary, as we pursue the will of God, we must pray. Generally speaking, the content of our prayers should be reflective of and driven by God's revelation of Himself in the Bible. More specifically, in Scripture we learn that we can pray for self-understanding and awareness of our own motives (see Psalm 139); we can intercede for others, including prayers regarding health and deliverance (see Jas. 5:13–16); we can pray for forgiveness (see 1 John 1:9); we can ask God for strength in the face of temptation (see Matt. 26:41); we can pray for effective evangelism (see Col. 4:2–4); we can ask God to meet our material needs (see Luke 11:9–10); we can pray for wisdom and insight into Scripture (see Jas. 1:5); and, among many other things, we can ask God for discernment and understanding (see Phil. 1:9–11). As we pray, then, God is pleased to grow us in Christ and to unfold His will.

The Holy Spirit and the Will of God

In discussions about God's will, questions often arise concerning the role of the Holy Spirit. In our survey of the contemporary and traditional views, we briefly noted that proponents of each of these models appeal to the ministry of the Holy Spirit in support of their position, albeit in different ways. In the preceding section on prayer and the will of God, we noted Paul's teaching at Rom. 8:27 that the "Spirit intercedes for the saints according to the will of God." Similarly, in the Psalms, David prayed, "Teach me to do your will, for you are my God! Let your good Spirit lead me on level ground!" (Ps. 143:10). Clearly, then, the Holy Spirit and the will of God are related, if not intertwined, subjects. In the discussion that follows we'll investigate the relationship between the Holy Spirit and believers' pursuit of the will of God.

Earlier in our study, we observed several narrative passages in the book of Acts where the Holy Spirit provided direct, individual guidance to believers about God's will. Among other examples, these included: the Holy Spirit sending Philip to converse with the Ethiopian eunuch (see Acts 8:29), the Holy Spirit directing Peter to visit with Cornelius (see Acts 10:19–20; 11:12), and the Holy Spirit setting Paul and Barnabas apart for ministry (see Acts 13:2).[7] As we noted, advocates of the contemporary model cite passages such as these in support of their view. Those who hold this position, then, believe it is normative for the Holy Spirit to give extra-biblical revelation to believers about God's will. However, in chapter three, we covered several problems related to making unique narrative passages, such as those cited above, a cornerstone in one's theology. Furthermore, we reviewed a number of challenges that accompany the practical denial of the doctrine of *sola Scriptura*, which occurs when we believe we need extra-biblical revelation to know and to do God's will.

In contrast to the contemporary view, advocates of the traditional view define the ministry of the Holy Spirit primarily in terms of guidance in biblical truth. Jesus repeatedly referred to the Holy Spirit as the "Spirit of Truth" (John 14:17; 15:26) and promised His disciples that the Holy Spirit "will guide you into all the truth" (John 16:13). In reading these verses it is possible to understand Christ to be teaching that the Holy Spirit will regularly give extra-biblical revelation to believers. However, we must not overlook the setting in which these passages occur. In the broader context, it is clear Jesus is preparing the disciples for His imminent departure. In this setting Christ teaches about the Holy Spirit and prays to the Father, "Sanctify them by Your truth. *Your word is truth*" (John 17:17; see Col. 1:5; 2 Tim. 2:15). Therefore, in stating that the coming Holy Spirit would guide believers into all truth, Jesus was teaching that the Holy Spirit's work would entail giving Christians an understanding of the Bible.[8] Theologians call this doctrine the Holy Spirit's ministry of illumination.

Of course, in his letters, Paul does refer to being "led by the Spirit" (Rom. 8:14; Gal. 5:18), "walk[ing] by the Spirit" (Gal. 5:16), and being "filled with the Spirit" (Eph. 5:18). At first glance, such references may seem to refer to individuals receiving supernatural guidance; however, upon closer examination it is clear Paul is not appealing to extra-biblical revelation in these verses. Rather, when read in context, it seems Paul is contrasting the effects of embracing one's own will with those of following God's will, as it is revealed in Scripture. In these passages Paul explains that to be led by, walk in, or be filled with the Holy Spirit will result in believers manifesting God's moral will, for they will "understand what the will of the Lord is" (Eph. 5:17).[9] Note that this phenomenon helps to explain the uniformity of Christian doctrine and practice over time and across cultures, for the Holy Spirit facilitates sanctification through the unchanging Word of God.

The primary work of the Holy Spirit, then, in regard to the will of God, is to illuminate the truth of Scripture, which reveals God's moral will. However, we ought not to overlook other roles fulfilled by the Holy Spirit that relate to the outworking of God's will in our lives. For example, in the Bible we learn that the Holy Spirit can empower for leadership (see Judg. 3:10; 1 Sam. 16:13), give intellectual insight and understanding (see Job 32:8), endow with artistic abilities (see Exod. 28:3; 31:3), provide gifts for ministry (see 1 Cor. 12:7–11), and comfort believers (see John 14:16). Furthermore, Scripture teaches that the Holy Spirit is responsible for the spiritual works of convicting of sin (see John 16:8), testifying about Jesus (see John 15:26), regenerating the lost (see John 6:63), as well as sanctifying believers (see Rom. 8:9–10). In all of these activities, the Holy Spirit unfolds God's moral and sovereign will and, in this process, creates fellowship and unity among believers within the Body of Christ (see Eph. 4:1–6).

Another area where the will of God and the Holy Spirit are often mentioned in the same context relates to experiencing a so-called "peace from God." To elaborate, some believers—especially those who hold to the contemporary view—assert that God guides Christians towards certain decisions by providing a supernatural peace about a particular option, choice, or action. To be sure, in his letter to the Philippian church, Paul does refer to a "peace of God, which surpasses all understanding, [which] will guard your hearts and your minds in Christ Jesus" (Phil. 4:6–7). Furthermore, in the book of Galatians, peace is identified as a fruit of the Holy Spirit (see Gal. 5:22). However, upon reading through all of the biblical passages that mention the Holy Spirit and divine peace,[10] we find that believers are never promised a subjective feeling of serenity that will guide them toward God's will. Rather, Scripture teaches that when Christians keep the revealed objective moral will of God, they can experience a peace that comes from the Holy Spirit (see Rom. 8:6). The peace of God, then, does not *lead toward* a hidden individual will of God, but *results from* a decision to follow the revealed moral will of God.

In summary, then, the ministry of the Holy Spirit in regard to God's will is primarily one of guidance in biblical truth. Paul taught the Corinthian church, "Now we have received not the spirit of the world, but the Spirit who is from God, that we might understand the things freely given us by God" (1 Cor. 2:12). This work of illumination by the Holy Spirit is essential for the sanctification of believers. Indeed, apart from the ministry of the Holy Spirit, Christians would not be able to understand God's revealed will, for divine truth seems like foolishness to natural man (see John 8:43; 1 Cor. 2:14; 1 John 5:6). As believers purpose to follow God's moral will, as revealed in Scripture, and to obey His Word, they can experience a peace from God, which is wrought by the Holy Spirit. Normatively speaking, then, the ministry of the Holy Spirit is not one of providing extra-biblical revelation, but one of guidance in the truth of Scripture.

Christian Liberty and the Will of God

In its most basic form, knowing and doing the will of God entails understanding God's moral will, as revealed in the Bible, and applying it to one's life. In regard to many subjects, this is relatively simple. For example, among other things, Scripture teaches that believers are to honor their parents, to uphold the sanctity of human life, and to abstain from sexual sin (see Exod. 20:12–14). In many ways, identifying and following these moral precepts seems elementary. However, experience teaches that understanding and applying God's moral law is not always clear-cut. This is sometimes due to the complexity of a given moral encounter, and at other times it is due to mitigating factors, such as the development of one's spiritual maturity, the presence of weaker brethren, or the sensitivity of one's conscience. Of course, this is not to say that God's moral law is subjective or that His moral will can change. Rather, it is to recognize that, at times, implementing the will of God in the fallen world can be a challenging task for imperfect human beings.

The idea that there is a degree of freedom in the

application—but not the content—of God's moral law is known as the doctrine of Christian liberty. This teaching relates to practices that are not explicitly prohibited, or specifically allowed, in the Bible. Thus, Christian liberty may include activities in which believers are free to engage; or, it may entail practices from which believers are free to abstain. Examples of areas where this teaching has been invoked in the past include: consuming alcohol, worship practices, music styles, games of chance, military service, places of employment, matters of commerce, eating practices, and the observance of special days, among many other issues. In each of these areas Christians have historically agreed that there is a degree of freedom in how the unchanging moral law of God is applied. As we'll explore in the discussion that follows, discerning the will of God in regard to such activities is not subjective; rather, it may be determined by considering a number of important, objective factors.

Oftentimes theologians will refer to practices that fall under the umbrella of Christian liberty as *adiaphora* issues. The term *adiaphora* literally means "things indifferent;" thus, activities related to Christian liberty are commonly understood to be morally indifferent in nature. Out of convention, we'll use the phrase "*adiaphora* issues" in the discussion that follows; however, we should note that this term is actually a misnomer, for in reality there are no morally indifferent practices. As I've argued elsewhere,[11] every volitional ethical event is either moral or immoral. This is why Paul instructs the believers in Colossae, "*Whatever you do*, in word or deed, do everything in the name of the Lord Jesus, giving thanks to God the Father through him" (Col. 3:17; see 1 Cor. 10:31). Properly understood, then, the doctrine of Christian liberty asserts that while certain activities may appear to be morally indifferent, God's will can always be determined by discerning the wisest application of the relevant, objective moral norms in a given context.

Weaker and Stronger Brethren

As we explored the traditional view in chapter 4, we noted the most important factor in determining the will of God, in any given situation, is to understand the relevant content of the Bible. Indeed, as has been noted, oftentimes knowing and doing God's will is as simple as applying Scripture to one's life. In regard to *adiaphora* issues, however, another factor that must be considered is the presence of weaker or stronger brethren. In fact, in the two most lengthy and significant passages in the Bible on the doctrine of Christian liberty, Rom. 14:1–15:13 and 1 Cor. 8:1–10:33,[12] Paul repeatedly exhorts believers to be mindful of the presence of weaker brethren. When engaging in morally indifferent activities, such a purposeful awareness and vigilance is a mark of neighbor-love. Since few people would self-identify as weaker brethren, Paul defines his categories within his discussion.

In mentioning weaker brethren, Paul characterizes such individuals as being weak in faith (see Rom. 14:1, 23), lacking full biblical knowledge (see 1 Cor. 8:1, 4, 7, 10–11), and having a fragile conscience (see 1 Cor. 8:7, 10–12; 10:28–29). However, from Paul's discussion, it is clear that a weaker brother is not any immature believer, a so-called carnal Christian,[13] or a believer who happens to disagree with an aspect of one's theology. Rather, in these passages a weaker brother is identified as someone who will be caused to violate their own conscience, in regard to an *adiaphora* issue, because of the influence and example of another Christian.[14] For the weaker brother, the sin here is not engaging in or abstaining from a particular act. Rather, it is the defilement of one's conscience (see Rom. 14:22–23). Among other possibilities, weaker brethren may include young children, recent converts, and believers from other countries, contexts, or cultures.

In Paul's epistles stronger brothers are described as individuals who have a mature faith (see Rom. 14:22), possess an abundance of scriptural knowledge (see 1 Cor. 8:1, 4, 7, 10–11), and have a biblically-informed conscience (see 1 Cor. 10:29–30). While we may be tempted to view a believer who is a meticulous law-keeper—that is, a legalist—as a stronger brother, ironically such individuals are actually described as weaker brethren in Scripture. Perhaps counter-intuitively, the Bible identifies the stronger brother as he who is without extra-biblical moral scruples. Indeed, stronger brethren exhibit a gracious freedom in Christ, for they understand that God's moral law is, as James wrote, "the law of liberty" (Jas. 1:25; 2:12) and that, as Jesus taught, "If the Son sets you free, you will be free indeed" (John 8:36).[15] Note, however, that in Scripture the stronger brother is always called to accommodate his actions—that is, to sacrifice his Christian liberty—for the sake of the weaker brother. This is because the stronger brother can do so without sinning, while the weaker brother can only accommodate his actions by violating his conscience and thereby sinning.

Christian Liberty and the Conscience

In the preceding discussion, the issue of one's conscience has been mentioned several times. Indeed, the conscience is a frequently cited concept in the Bible, and it is an important component in the process of knowing and doing God's will. Scripture describes the conscience in various ways. Positively, the Bible speaks of having a "good conscience" (Acts 23:1; 1 Tim. 1:5, 19; 1 Pet. 3:21), a "clear conscience" (Acts 24:16; 1 Tim. 3:9; 2 Tim. 1:3; Heb. 13:18; see 1 Pet. 3:16), a cleansed conscience (see Heb. 9:14), and a conscience without guilt (see Rom 9:1; 1 Cor. 4:4; 2 Cor. 1:12). Negatively, Scripture mentions the possibility of an "evil conscience" (Heb. 10:22), a defiled conscience (see Titus 1:15; Heb. 9:9), a weak conscience (see 1 Cor. 8:7, 10), as well as a seared conscience (see 1 Tim. 4:2).

Whether it is functioning positively or negatively, the conscience can be defined as the component of the human constitution that bears witness to the morality of actions (see Rom. 2:15). The conscience communicates an inherent moral ought-ness that stems from man being made in the image of God. In a perfect world the conscience would accurately and comprehensively reflect God's moral will. However, since the fall of man, the conscience has been susceptible to being co-opted by sin. This is because the conscience is informed by the mind (or the intellect) and the mind is part of the fallen fleshly body (see 1 Cor. 4:3–4; Eph. 2:1–3). While believers receive a new immaterial nature at the moment of conversion, they must wait for a new material body until their resurrection at the return of Christ. Consequently, prior to glorification, Christians must wrestle with the sinful flesh, which includes the mind (see Rom. 7:13–25). Additionally, the conscience is continually being conditioned by one's experiences, which are oftentimes sinful in the context of the fallen world.

The fact that the conscience can be misled by the fallen mind, and misaligned on account of sinful experiences, means that it is possible for one's conscience to be wrong. In Pauline terminology, an individual whose conscience has been misinformed in regard to an *adiaphora* issue is a "weaker brother." Concerning morally indifferent practices, when a stronger brother causes a weaker brother to violate his conscience—even though the weaker brother's conscience is incorrect—it is a sinful act. In such cases the stronger brother, in effect, encourages the weaker brother to disregard his conscience (see Rom. 14:23). This is wrong, for in regard to non-morally indifferent practices, the weaker brother needs to follow his conscience. The possibility of this phenomena highlights the need for all believers to be aware of the presence of weaker brethren and to be continually filling, training, and programing (or, perhaps, re-programming) their minds with the truth of the Word of God. Paul touched upon and exemplified this idea as he claimed, "My conscience bears me witness in the Holy Spirit" (Rom. 9:1).

Principles of Christian Liberty

In regard to *adiaphora* issues, familiarity with the Bible, awareness of the presence of weaker brethren, and being sensitive to the conscience are indispensable components of knowing and doing the will of God. In light of these factors, we can summarize a general approach to morally indifferent practices with several principles of Christian liberty.

First, no one should impose their own moral scruples upon another in regard to morally indifferent practices. We must keep in mind the fact that God is the ultimate Judge of mankind, not man. Paul instructed the believers in Rome, "Therefore let us not pass judgment on one another any longer, but rather decide never to put a stumbling block or hindrance in the way of a brother" (Rom. 14:13). This means that Christians who engage in morally indifferent practices ought not to despise those who do not (see Rom. 14:1; 15:1). Likewise, those who abstain from *adiaphora* activities must not judge those who do (see Rom. 14:3). All such practices should be rooted in a godly mind (see Rom. 12:1–2; Phil. 4:8).

Second, those who engage in morally indifferent practices must be convinced in their own minds that such acts are helpful to the Body of Christ, realizing that we all will be judged for our actions (see Rom. 14:5, 12, 14, 23). In writing about *adiaphora* issues at 1 Cor. 6:12 Paul noted, "'All things are lawful for me,' but not all things are helpful. 'All things are lawful for me,' but I will not be dominated by anything." Similarly, at 1 Cor. 10:23 Paul wrote, "'All things are lawful,' but not all things are helpful. 'All things are lawful,' but not all things build up" (see Rom. 15:2). Morally indifferent practices, then, must be profitable for oneself and for others, and ought not to enslave mankind—be it physically, emotionally, or spiritually.

Third, morally indifferent practices must be done unto the Lord—that is, in service to God, exalting God, and for the glory of God (see Rom. 14:6–8; 15:6–7; 1 Cor. 6:13; 10:31). In other words, *adiaphora* practices should be done in Jesus' name, and one ought to be able to thank Him for it (see Col. 3:17). This means that morally indifferent practices must be appropriate for the body, which is the temple of the Holy Spirit. Paul instructed the Corinthian believers, "Do you not know that your body is a temple of the Holy Spirit? . . . You are not your own, for you were bought with a price. So glorify God in your body" (1 Cor. 6:19–20).

Fourth, morally indifferent practices must not become a stumbling block for weaker brothers (see Rom. 14:13, 15, 20–21). Paul cautioned the Corinthian church, "But take care that this right of yours does not somehow become a stumbling block to the weak. . . . And so by your knowledge this weak person is destroyed, the brother for whom Christ died. Thus, sinning against your brothers and wounding their conscience when it is weak, you sin against Christ" (1 Cor. 8:9–12). *Adiaphora* acts, then, ought not to tear down, but should promote peace, joy, love, edification, and even evangelism among the members of the Body of Christ (see Rom. 14:17, 19; 15:8–13; 1 Cor. 8:1; 10:31–33).

Fifth, as has been noted above, a morally indifferent act becomes sinful for a believer if it causes him to transgress his conscience. As he wrote about *adiaphora* practices, Paul taught, "I know and am persuaded in the Lord Jesus that nothing is unclean in itself, but it is unclean for anyone who thinks it unclean" (Rom. 14:14). In this passage, Paul was not teaching that morality is subjective; rather, he was highlighting the importance of not violating one's conscience. Paul later stated the same truth differently as he claimed, "For whatever does not proceed from faith is sin" (Rom. 14:23). John, too, expressed this idea as he wrote, "If our heart does not condemn us, we have confidence before God" (1 John 3:21).

Sixth, a stronger brother must always be willing to sacrifice his Christian liberty for the sake of a weaker brother (see 1 Cor. 8:13; 10:28–29). Indeed, a truly mature Christian is strong enough to sacrifice his freedom for the welfare of and service to a weaker brother. In regard to morally indifferent practices, an unwillingness to accommodate one's actions for the sake of a fellow Christian is a sure sign that one is, in fact, a weaker brother. Regarding this principle, Paul's exhortation to the Galatian believers is helpful, as he writes, "For you were called to freedom, brothers. Only do not use your freedom as an opportunity for the flesh, but through love serve one another" (Gal. 5:13).

Seventh, the one who engages in morally indifferent practices must act in imitation of Jesus, for He is Lord (see Rom. 14:9). Paul concluded his discussion of *adiaphora* issues in the book of Romans, writing, "We who are strong have an obligation to bear with the failings of the weak, and not to please ourselves. Let each of us please his neighbor for his good, to build him up. For Christ did not please himself. . . . Therefore welcome one another as Christ has welcomed you, for the glory of God" (Rom. 15:1–3, 7). In short, then, as is the case with other areas of Christian living, so in regard to Christian liberty, believers must imitate Christ.

Conclusion

In this chapter we have explored the relationship between prayer and the will of God, the role of the Holy Spirit in making moral decisions, and the place of Christian liberty in knowing and doing God's will. In regard to prayer, we saw that prayer is a vital discipline for believers. While Christians ought not to expect extra-biblical revelation in prayer, the discipline of prayer is essential for fostering one's relationship with God and understanding God's moral will. Moreover, prayer is not contrary to God's sovereign will but is a part of it. We also saw that oftentimes the Holy Spirit works in prayer to guide believers in understanding the truth of Scripture. This illuminating ministry of the Holy Spirit is sometimes accompanied by a peace from God that comes when one obeys God's Word. Finally, we saw that Christian liberty affords believers a degree of freedom in the application of God's moral will concerning *adiaphora* issues. As we noted, in regard to morally indifferent practices, Christians must be aware of the presence of weaker brethren and be sensitive to the conscience.

Summary Points

• Advocates of both the contemporary and traditional views appeal to prayer, the Holy Spirit, and Christian liberty; however, each model understands these components of Christian living differently.

• Proponents of the traditional view understand prayer to be an expression of one's faith, trust, and love for God. The discipline is primarily about communing with God around His Word, not getting extra-biblical communication from God.

• The primary role of the Holy Spirit is one of guiding in the truth of Scripture. While the Holy Spirit did give extra-biblical guidance to God's people in the Bible on rare occasions, and is free to do so today, Christians are never taught to expect such occurrences.

• Christian liberty is the idea that, in regard to morally indifferent practices, there is a degree of freedom in how the moral will of God is applied. Activities that fall under the umbrella of Christian liberty are sometimes called *adiaphora* practices.

Two of the most important factors to consider in discerning the will of God in regard to morally indifferent practices are the presence of weaker brethren and the sensitivity of one's conscience.

CHAPTER 6:
CONCLUSION AND APPLICATION

As our study of knowing and doing the will of God draws to a close, we ought to reiterate the fact that the focus of this book has been upon constructing a normative path for Christian living. In other words, the aim of this volume has been to trace and to synthesize the information in the Bible that specifically informs believers concerning how to pursue and to obey the will of God. As we've noted several times over the previous chapters, God is free to reveal His will in any way He pleases, including the use of supernatural means. Indeed, Scripture reports that from time-to-time in the biblical era God did reveal His will in extraordinary ways. Moreover, there are accounts in church history of God using miraculous means to disclose His will. However, in constructing an orthodox theology of God's will, the best practice is to focus upon that which is prescribed, standard, and normative in the Bible, not events that are exceptional, anomalous, or singular. Indeed, the majority of the Christian life occurs on the regular paths and according to the general patterns that God has set forth in Scripture.

By way of summary and review, after reading the material in the preceding five chapters we can reach a number of conclusions. First, we can confidently assert that the will of God is an important topic for followers of Christ, for this subject is mentioned frequently in the Bible. As we noted in chapter 1, the concept of the will of God is specifically cited dozens of times in Scripture, and the general idea of God's will is present in hundreds of passages. In surveying the various biblical references to the will of God it is evident that there are two main ways in which the concept is used in Scripture. In some passages God's sovereign will is in view, which is the idea that God has eternally decreed all things that come to pass. In other passages, the Bible addresses God's moral will, which entails the moral standards that have been revealed by God to mankind. When God's moral will is applied in one's own life, we can call this God's individual will; however, this category does not normatively exist apart from God's moral will, nor is it more specific than God's moral will. Whether God's sovereign will or His moral will is in view, then, the recurrence of the theme of God's will in Scripture testifies to the importance of this topic for followers of Christ.

Second, throughout history it is clear that mankind has pursued the will of God using a variety of means of revelation—or, at least, attempts at receiving revelation. In chapter 2 we surveyed several pagan methodologies for discerning God's will that are described in the Bible. Among other practices, these means of divination included false prophets, casting of lots, interpretation of dreams, and astrology. We also reviewed a number of biblical methodologies of revelation that were used by God in the narrative of Scripture to reveal His will. These means included true prophets, casting of lots, dreams and visions, and supernatural signs, among a number of other practices and special events. In our survey it was perhaps surprising to see some overlap between pagan means of divination and biblical methodologies of revelation. Yet, regardless of the pagan or biblical nature of the practices that were utilized, we noted that these events were so infrequent in Scripture—whether legitimately employed or not—that they are unlikely to be of much help in the modern church.

Third, in chapter 3 we saw that many Christians pursue the will of God in ways that are strikingly similar to pagan methodologies of divination or to the exceptional means of revelation that God used in the Bible. This approach, which we called the contemporary view, consists of looking for agreement between various means of revelation, including Scripture, prayer, personal counsel, individual desires, circumstances, personal peace, and various supernatural signs. While some of these methodologies are helpful, we noted the tendency of many advocates of the contemporary view to focus upon subjective feelings of personal peace and/or the perceived reception of supernatural signs. As we observed, this reliance upon extra-biblical revelation for divine guidance often rests upon selective methods of Bible interpretation and has historically led to distortions in the doctrines of God, sanctification, and Scripture. In sum, we found the contemporary model for discerning God's will to be wanting and, perhaps, in some ways to be outside the bounds of orthodoxy.

The many challenges that accompany the contemporary view left us looking for a less problematic approach to knowing and doing the will of God. This, in turn, led us to a fourth conclusion—that is, we can know God's will with confidence by studying Scripture. This idea, which we labeled the traditional view, focuses on knowing the contents of the Bible and applying the moral precepts of Scripture to everyday life. In chapter 4 we observed the place of biblical wisdom within this historical model, as we defined wisdom as the practical application of God's Word to daily living. In short, then, the traditional view encourages believers to know the Bible so that they will be able to live their lives in accord with its contents. In our study we observed that there are different ways to learn and to understand the contents of Scripture, including Bible reading, Bible study, memorizing Scripture, and receiving biblical counsel, among the observance of other classic spiritual disciplines.

A fifth conclusion, which is related to the traditional view, is that prayer, the Holy Spirit, and Christian liberty play important roles in knowing and doing the will of God. Concerning prayer, in chapter 5 we noted that this practice is best understood to be an expression of one's faith, trust, and love for God. Whereas God speaks to believers through the Bible, believers can speak to God through prayer. Prayer, then, is not primarily about getting extra-biblical messages from God; rather, it is about responding to God's self-revelation in His Word and calibrating one's relationship with God. The Holy Spirit aids in this process as He illuminates Scripture, thus guiding God's people in truth and helping believers to understand God's revealed moral will. We observed that obeying God's moral will is often straightforward; however, in regard to morally indifferent practices, the application of Scripture is sometimes more challenging. As we noted, concerning matters of Christian liberty, the most important factors to consider are knowing the contents of Scripture, maintaining an awareness of the presence of weaker brethren, and being sensitive to conscience—both one's own conscience and the consciences of others.

Applying God's Will

Toward the end of chapter 4 we suggested several steps for implementing the traditional model of knowing and doing the will of God. As we head toward the conclusion of this study, it may be helpful to briefly work through an example of how to pursue and to apply God's will, utilizing our earlier suggestions. For illustration purposes, let's consider the case of someone who is unhappy in their current job and is considering changing places of employment or even switching careers altogether.

Using the aforementioned paradigm, a good first step in considering a change of employment would be to study any relevant scriptural passages on work, labor, vocation, and related issues, for these teachings will reveal the moral will of God. This biblical material may be as broad as verses about the goodness of work (see Eccl. 9:9–10; Col. 3:23–24), the need to work (see 1 Tim. 5:8; 2 Thess. 3:10), and the results of work (see Prov. 12:24; 14:23). Further, it may be helpful to review specific scriptural material on topics related to one's vocation, such as teachings on contentment (see Phil. 4:12–13; 1 Tim. 6:6–7), diligence (see Prov. 13:4; Gal. 6:9), and even personal finance (see Prov. 22:7; Rom. 13:8). As we discussed earlier, when considering God's will in regard to a particular subject, there are many ways to digest the relevant material in Scripture, including Bible reading, listening to sermons, and receiving biblical counsel, among other means.

A second step in discerning the will of God in regard to a possible job transition is to pray. As we've previously noted, the main purpose of prayer is not to get extra-biblical revelation, but to properly align or calibrate one's relationship with God. When believers draw near to God they can be helped by the Holy Spirit in understanding the truth of God's Word. Furthermore, as we meditate upon God's Word, we can pray for wisdom (see Jas. 1:5), self-understanding (see Ps. 139:23–24), and discernment (see Phil. 1:9–11), among other more specific requests (see Phil. 4:5–6). A decision regarding a possible job change, whether it be to a new employer or to a completely new industry, can naturally cause apprehension and anxiety. However, through the disciplines of Bible intake and prayer, we can orient our hearts and minds toward God so that we can affirm with David, "I have calmed and quieted my soul, like a weaned child with its mother; like a weaned child is my soul within me" (Ps. 131:2). Such a disposition will better enable us to know and to do God's moral will.

In our current example, a third step in pursing God's will would be to consider our own gifts, abilities, opportunities, and God-given desires. In chapter 4 we noted that the best course of action is always the one that is most spiritually expedient. Concerning a potential job change, then, it would be appropriate to ask questions such as: Are my spiritual gifts, natural abilities, and life experiences being utilized properly in my current job? Would I be able to accomplish more Kingdom work in a different setting? Is my desire for a job change being driven by a longing to better steward my gifts and abilities, to gain more status and money, or for some other reason? Is my heart properly aligned with God, so that His desires have become my desires? Ultimately, the best way forward in regard to a possible job transition is to consider the optimal use of one's spiritual gifts, natural abilities, life experiences, educational preparation, and present opportunities. The ideal balance between these factors is often an indicator of the path that is most spiritually expedient.

A fourth step in seeking God's will concerning a possible career change would be to seek advice from other mature believers, especially one's spiritual leaders and those who have gone through similar life experiences in the past. As we noted earlier, it is wise to receive biblical counsel from other Christians about God's will. Such advice might consist of an explanation, from a more mature saint, of how the Bible speaks to a particular issue with which we are grappling. However, we can also get practical, common-sense advice from other believers about life issues. Such counsel would naturally arise out of a Christian worldview, yet it might not be as specific as applying a Bible verse to one's life. The idea here is that the Body of Christ can be mutually self-serving, in a beneficial sense, as wisdom, theology, and life experience is shared (see Prov. 27:17). Indeed, imitating the lives of mature believers who have a firm grasp of Scripture will result in our own sanctification. Observe Jeremiah's advice to God's people, "Thus says the LORD: 'Stand by the roads, and look, and ask for the ancient paths, where the good way is; and walk in it, and find rest for your souls'" (Jer. 6:16).

Finally, in considering a career change, we must evaluate the effects of such a decision upon others. In the Bible we are repeatedly exhorted to love our neighbors as ourselves (see Matt. 22:39; Gal. 5:14). In fact, both Jesus and Paul teach that neighbor-love is an essential component of keeping God's moral will (see Matt. 22:39–40; Rom. 13:9–10). A decision as weighty as a job transition will undoubtedly have an effect upon our neighbors, which includes our family members, co-workers, and friends. Given the impact upon those closest to us, then, one contemplating a career transition would be wise to carefully consider if such a move is the best course of action for all parties involved. Recall our earlier observation from 1 Cor. 6:12; 10:23 where Paul taught that just because something is permitted, does not mean that it is always the right choice. Indeed, the best course of action can only be determined by considering all of the pertinent factors.

After considering the above biblically-rooted suggestions, the final step for one considering a job change is to confidently make a decision to the glory of God (see Isa. 43:7; 1 Cor. 10:31). Of course, spending time working through the above steps in seeking God's will may not be as exciting as receiving extra-biblical revelation, nor does it carry the spiritual cachet of following subjective feelings of supernatural guidance. Yet, in seeking to know and to do God's will, such a biblically grounded approach to Christian living is more likely to result in a decision that will be useful to the church, fulfilling to oneself, and glorifying to God.

Living God's Will

In concluding our study, a brief word needs to be said about living out and discussing God's will within the Body of Christ. In this book we have considered two broad models of knowing and doing the will of God. Undoubtedly, as we engage in church life, we'll come across individuals who have different views on this topic than ourselves. In light of the varying views among believers on this issue, we'd be wise to winsomely accept and to gently exhort brethren whose understanding of the will of God is different from our own. This is not to say that we overlook what we might perceive to be an incorrect or even a harmful perspective. Rather, it is to recognize that divergent views on God's will ought not to be a test of Christian fellowship—as long as they fall within the realm of Christian orthodoxy. Indeed, as in all areas where believers disagree, the best course of action is to gather together around God's Word and to let it shape our theology and to nourish our relationship with God and with one another.

Finally, as we discuss God's will with other believers, we must be aware of and careful about the language we use. Take, for example, the instance of a pastor declaring that it is God's will for a church to embark upon a building campaign to construct a new sanctuary. Many church members might interpret such a statement to mean that God has supernaturally instructed the pastor to lead the church into a new building project. However, in stating his belief that it is God's will to build a new sanctuary, the pastor may actually mean to communicate that, as the overseer of a growing church, after praying to God with Scripture in hand, he believes the best stewardship of the church's resources and opportunities is to consider constructing a larger sanctuary. These divergent understandings are each a reasonable interpretation of an ambiguous reference to God's will. Thus, in light of the possibility of such confusion, it is important that we make every effort to communicate clearly what we mean when we speak about God's will.

Conclusion

In this volume, we've covered a lot of ground in our study of knowing and doing God's will. As was noted in the preface to this book, oftentimes it is difficult to analyze our past choices, for it is easy to spot errors that we have made, as we are all often prone to confuse our will with God's will. Yet, despite the unwise or even sinful decisions that we've made in the past, we can be comforted in knowing that God abounds with grace, love, and forgiveness for his children. While we cannot undo yesterday's unwise decisions, we can always repent of our former sinful choices and purpose to follow God today. May we all display the same patience toward others that God has repeatedly shown toward us. As you continue to follow God's revealed will for your life, it is my prayer that the beauty and the sufficiency of Scripture will captivate your heart and your mind.

Summary Points

• God is free to reveal His will in any way He chooses, including supernatural means; however, in constructing a theology of God's will, the best practice is to focus upon that which is prescribed, standard, and normative in the Bible.

• The will of God is an important and recurring theme in Scripture, as the Bible speaks both of God's sovereign will, which entails everything that comes to pass, and of God's moral will, which includes the moral standards revealed by God in His Word.

• We can know God's will most clearly and confidently by studying the Bible. There are different ways to digest the content of Scripture, including Bible study, memorizing Scripture, and receiving biblical counsel, among other Bible-centric means.

• In speaking about and living out God's will within the Body of Christ, we must gently and patiently exhort brethren with divergent views, seeking to let the Word of God give shape to all of our theology.

• Given various views on the topic within the church, in discussions about the will of God, there is a danger of miscommunication; therefore, we must strive to clearly communicate our beliefs and intentions when speaking about God's will.

FREQUENTLY ASKED QUESTIONS

As was noted in the preface to this book, my goal in writing this text has been to point believers toward the beauty, truth, and sufficiency of the Scriptures. As you've read through this volume, I pray that your love for God and His Holy Word has grown. In teaching this material in the past, I've learned that exploring what the Bible teaches about knowing and doing the will of God can sometimes generate as many questions as it answers. In view of this phenomenon, in this brief appendix, I've tried to address some of the most frequently asked questions that have arisen as I've taught on this important subject over the years.

- **Doesn't the traditional view make God seem cold and distant?**

Upon learning the traditional view for the first time, some people feel that this teaching makes God seem cold and distant, as if Christianity were a form of deism. This is especially true for believers who have followed a more mystical approach to knowing and doing the will of God in the past. This phenomenon can be explained in that some followers of the contemporary view errantly equate their perceived reception of extra-biblical revelation (e.g., personal peace, supernatural signs, etc.) with intimacy with God. Since the traditional view understands extra-biblical revelation to be non-normative, this view then seems to depict God as being cold and distant. In actuality, however, the perception of receiving extra-biblical revelation does not require intimacy with God or even knowledge of God. In contrast, as this book has explored, the traditional view teaches that in order to know and to do the will of God, individuals must have an intimate relationship with God that is fostered by an ever-growing knowledge of His Word. This is essential for Christian maturity, as "faith comes by hearing, and hearing by the word of God" (Rom. 10:17, NKJV). As believers grow in their intimacy with God, through the revelation of God's Word, they cultivate the mind of Christ (see 1 Cor. 2:16).

- **Does looking to extra-biblical sources for knowledge of God's will really contradict the doctrine of *sola Scriptura*?**

As was mentioned earlier, Protestant Christians have historically held to the doctrine of *sola Scriptura*. This is the teaching that the Word of God is sufficient for Christian faith and practice. As we explored the contemporary view in this book, it was suggested that looking to extra-biblical sources for knowledge of God's will contradicts this key Protestant doctrine. Indeed, this is true, for if one believes that it is *essential* to look to extra-biblical sources for knowledge of God's will, then it must be the case that God's Word is not sufficient for Christian faith and practice. Note that the doctrine of *sola Scriptura* ought not to be confused with the error of *solo Scriptura,* which holds that God cannot reveal His will apart from the Scriptures. As traditional view advocates explain, God is free to reveal Himself in any way He so chooses at any time; yet, as the Bible teaches, the normative way that God has chosen to reveal Himself to His people is through His written Word. We must remember that discussions about knowing and doing the will of God ought not to be centered upon what

God *can* do, but upon what God *does* do. In other words, doctrine needs to be rooted in what is normative, not in what is exceptional. While God is always free to act exceptionally, to expect regular extra-biblical revelation makes exceptional revelation normative and infringes upon the sufficiency of Scripture.

- **Are the contemporary and traditional views mutually exclusive, or are other views possible? Can someone hold to a hybrid position that combines these two views?**

Over time, as Christians have considered knowing and doing the will of God, the contemporary and traditional views have been the two main options that have arisen—although believers have used different terminology to describe these two positions. If one were to conceive of these views as being on opposite ends of a spectrum, it would be logically possible to hold to an infinite number of positions between these two options. It seems that one of the main differences between the contemporary and traditional views is one's source of authority. Since advocates of both the contemporary and the traditional view affirm God's freedom to act supernaturally, as well as the importance of Scripture, it seems that that which would differentiate any hybrid position on a continuum between these two views would be related to one's source of authority. To elaborate, in practice, contemporary view advocates give more authority to one's personal experience of the supernatural, while traditional view advocates place more emphasis upon the sufficiency of the written Word of God. Any hybrid view, then, would likely be determined by the way in which one leans regarding a source of authority, as well as one's understanding of what the Bible reveals as being normative in the Christian life.

- **Do advocates of the traditional view believe that God has no individual will for Christians?**

As was mentioned several times in this volume, traditional view advocates *do* believe and readily affirm that God has an individual will for every person. However, such advocates define the individual will of God as the moral will of God applied in the life of a Christian. So, both followers of the contemporary view and the traditional view assert that God has an individual will for every person. The difference is that contemporary view advocates believe that God's individual will is hidden and revealed extra-biblically, while traditional view advocates assert that God's individual will is evident and revealed biblically. To return to the opening illustration of this book regarding marriage: contemporary view advocates teach that John will know if he should marry Jennifer only if God reveals it to him extra-biblically (i.e., via personal peace, a supernatural sign, etc.). Traditional view advocates teach that Scripture reveals John should marry a believer (see 2 Cor. 6:14). Since Jennifer is a believer, John is free to marry her, as this would be an application of God's moral will to his individual life. As Paul wrote to the Corinthians, John "is free to be married to whom [he] wishes, only in the Lord" (1 Cor. 7:39).

- **What about the relationship between ministerial callings and the will of God?**

Ephesians 4:11–12 teaches that God gifts or calls ministerial leaders to the church in order to equip believers and to edify the Body of Christ. From these verses, as well as from similar passages (i.e., Rom. 12:6–8; 1 Cor. 12:29–30; 1 Pet. 4:10–11), it seems clear that ministerial capacity is the result of spiritual giftedness. Of course, there are narratives in Scripture where God works in supernatural, extra-biblical ways to appoint people into vocational ministry and/or to make individuals aware of their spiritual giftedness. New Testament examples include Paul (see Acts 9:1–19) and Timothy (see 1 Tim. 1:18; 4:14). While God certainly could work via special revelation in order to call individuals into ministry today, this is not the normative pattern in the New Testament. Rather, all believers receive spiritual gift(s) at their salvation (see Rom. 12:6; 1 Cor. 7:7; 12:11), with some being given gifts related to ministerial leadership, such as pastors, teachers, evangelists, etc. As with all spiritual gifts, when believers grow in maturity, so will their desire to use their spiritual gift(s) for the good of the church (see 1 Cor. 12:7; 1 Pet. 4:10). This explains why, when writing to Timothy, Paul begins his instructions on pastoral qualifications with the teaching, "If a man *desires* the position of a bishop, he *desires* a good thing" (1 Tim. 3:1, NKJV). Normatively speaking, then, ministerial calling can be equated with a desire for ministerial service that arises out of spiritual giftedness that is empowered by the Holy Spirit (see 1 Cor. 12:7). Of course, just because someone desires to lead in ministry does not mean that they have been so gifted. This is why Paul gives a host of characteristics for ministerial leaders that the church can use to recognize and, perhaps, even to ordain individuals who have such a giftedness (see 1 Tim. 3:1–13; Titus 1:5–9). Since there is much opportunity to be misunderstood when speaking about ministerial callings, believers ought to be careful to define the terms they use when speaking about church leadership.

- **What about reports from the mission field about miracles, healings, dreams, visions, and other supernatural events?**

Throughout history, there are many recorded instances, especially from the mission field, of God using Christians to facilitate miracles and healings, as well as to perform other supernatural signs. In fact, in the late twentieth and early twenty-first century there have been many accounts of God moving unbelievers toward salvation in Jesus Christ via dreams and visions, especially in traditional Muslim countries. In many respects, these supernatural occurrences are parallel to events recorded in the book of Acts. While some have suggested that these extraordinary occurrences are incompatible with the traditional view, advocates of this position suggest that these events actually support the traditional view, along the following lines: first, accounts of supernatural events from the mission field are not normative, but exceptional, even where they are occurring; second, as was the case in the biblical era, so it is today that reports of supernatural events tend to be from foreign lands where people lack access to the Bible in their native language; third, just like in the book of Acts, the pattern throughout history has been that once the church is established in an area, supernatural signs diminish as people gain access to the superior revelation of the Word of God.

- **How should Christians handle *adiaphora* issues over which a particular stance is taken by an individual, a church, or other institution?**

In our discussion about Christian liberty, we noted that some topics are not directly addressed by Scripture. Over time, believers have adopted differing stances on such issues. These morally indifferent topics (e.g., worship styles, consuming alcohol, military service, etc.) are commonly referred to as *adiaphora* issues. In our consideration of Christian liberty, we suggested several principles to consider when weighing morally indifferent practices. While we may realize that others can legitimately adopt different positions on *adiaphora* issues, this invites the question as to how to interact with those with whom we disagree on a morally indifferent subject, especially if they are our leaders. In short, if we have placed ourselves under the authority of an individual or an organization with whom we disagree on an *adiaphora* issue, the best way forward is to submit to such an individual or an organization. This is so, for it is always sinful to rebel against authority, unless doing so is going to cause us to sin or keep us from righteousness. By definition, *adiaphora* issues are morally indifferent; therefore, conforming to the stance of an individual over us, or an organization of which we are a part, ought not to cause us to sin or keep us from righteousness.

- **How should Christians interact with other believers who disagree with their view of the will of God?**

In any group of Christians who are discussing the will of God, it is likely that differing views of this topic will be present. In short, many in the modern church who have not studied this issue in depth, as well as those given toward a more mystical form of Christianity, will often hold to the contemporary view, while other believers may lean toward the traditional view. In thinking through Christ-like interaction between believers who disagree on this issue, it is important to keep two things in mind. First, while the will of God is an important and practical topic for Christians, it is not what scholars would consider to be a first-tier theological doctrine. Examples of first-tier theological doctrines include things like justification by faith alone, the deity of Christ, and Jesus' resurrection from the dead, among many others. Orthodox believers must agree on these clear biblical teachings, as they are foundational issues for the Christian faith. The will of God, however, is what could be called a second-tier theological doctrine. Other second-tier theological doctrines include subjects such as the timing of Jesus' return, the proper mode of baptism, and the best form of church government. These topics, while still important, are issues about which Christians have historically disagreed and over which believers ought not to sever fellowship. Therefore, Christians can disagree about the will of God and still charitably discuss their differences. Second, it is important that believers not only have doctrinal beliefs, but also that they know why they believe what they believe. Indeed, in regard to second-tier theological issues we must always be willing to hold our beliefs up to the light of Scripture, to consider competing views, and to adjust our perspectives as is necessary. In summary, then, we ought to expect that there will be disagreement among Christians about the will of God. Yet, such divergence of thought is not a reason to part company with another believer; rather, it is an opportunity to explain our position, to examine our beliefs, to explore the views of others, and possibly to find common ground or, at a minimum, to gain a better understanding of alternative theological viewpoints.

- **What if I've made major life decisions in the past utilizing what I now believe to be an unbiblical model of moral decision making?**

As Christians mature in their faith, it is not uncommon for someone to move from a mystical view of moral decision making to a perspective that is more biblically grounded. Should this happen, there is no need to dwell upon or to become obsessed with past life decisions. As is the case with all of life, God always accepts us where he finds us. The duty required of all mankind, whether believers or unbelievers, is to repent of our sins, being confident, "If we confess our sins, he is faithful and just to forgive us our sins and to cleanse us from all unrighteousness" (1 John 1:9). Of course, there is no need to repent of non-sinful past choices and decisions, even if they were made utilizing a model that one now believes to be incorrect. Indeed, on account of Christians' general knowledge of God's moral law, often believers realize that they have made good life decisions in the past, even if they did so with incorrect motives or while employing a model of decision making that they now believe to be insufficient. Remember that the individual will of God for all people is the application of the moral will of God in one's life.

- **What are some critiques and/or distortions of the traditional view?**

It will be clear to readers of this book that I am an advocate of the traditional view, as I find this position to be the view most in harmony with the Scriptures. Moreover, the traditional view is certainly the historical position of the church. Yet, the traditional view is not without critiques, for if it was, there would not be debate among Bible-believing Christians as to how to know and to do the will of God. The most common critique of the traditional view is that in emphasizing the priority of Scripture in knowing God's will, it may lead some people to practically deny that God can reveal Himself supernaturally, which is an error. Another critique of the traditional view is that, given the emphasis upon the Bible, this position may lead some people to wrongly become legalistic in their thoughts and actions. A legalist is someone who keeps the letter of the law, solely for the sake of law-keeping, without a love for God and for His people. Finally, a third critique of the traditional view is that it may overlook the fact that when someone is inquiring about the will of God, they are usually asking a very personal and intimate question. Wise advocates of the traditional view will be aware of these critiques and pastorally walk inquirers through a personal application of the will of God as is revealed in His Word.

SUGGESTED READING

In an attempt to make this book more readable, I have purposely not cited any other volumes in the text of the preceding discussion. Any interaction with resources, or other expansion of thought, has been suppressed to the endnotes, which I pray you will find helpful. There are, however, a number of influential works that have shaped my own thinking in regard to the will of God. I would commend the following books to readers who are interested in further exploring the topics considered in this volume.

Barclay, Oliver B. *Guidance: What the Bible Says about Knowing God's Will.* Downers Grove, IL: InterVarsity, 1978.

Bloomfield, Peter. *What the Bible Teaches about Guidance.* Webster, NY: Evangelical Press, 2006.

Friesen, Garry. *Decision Making and the Will of God.* Eugene, OR: Multnomah, 2009.

Challies, Tim. *The Discipline of Spiritual Discernment.* Wheaton: Crossway, 2007.

DeYoung, Kevin. *Just Do Something: A Liberating Approach to Finding God's Will. Or How to Make a Decision Without Dreams, Visions, Fleeces, Open Doors, Random Bible Verses, Casting Lots, Liver Shivers, Writing in the Sky, etc.* Chicago: Moody, 2014.

DeYoung, Kevin. *Taking God at His Word: Why the Bible Is Knowable, Necessary, and Enough, and What That Means for You and Me.* Wheaton, IL: Crossway, 2016.

Huffman, Douglas S. *How Then Should We Choose? Three Views on God's Will and Decision Making.* Grand Rapids: Kregel, 2009.

Jensen, Philip D., and Tony Payne. *Guidance and the Voice of God.* Kingsford, Australia: Matthias Media, 1997.

MacArthur, John, *Found: God's Will.* Colorado Springs, CO: David C. Cook, 2012.

Waltke, Bruce K. *Finding the Will of God: A Pagan Notion?* 2d. ed. Grand Rapids: Eerdmans, 2016.

QUESTIONS FOR GROUP STUDY

Chapter 1

1. Why are so many Christians interested in the topic of knowing and doing the will of God?
2. What are some disingenuous or even dangerous reasons why some people—even some believers—desire to know God's will?
3. What is God's sovereign will? Can anyone know God's sovereign will before it occurs? If so, how?
4. What is God's moral will? How can we know God's moral will? How does God's moral will relate to His sovereign will?
5. What is God's individual will? How does God's individual will relate to His sovereign will and His moral will?

Chapter 2

1. How can we know that God will guide His followers? In what ways has God promised to give guidance to believers?
2. In Scripture, in what ways did pagans attempt to get divine guidance? Have you ever witnessed such attempts at divination?
3. In the Bible, in what ways did God choose to reveal His will to mankind? What methodologies of divine revelation are most attractive to you?

4. Are events such as angelic visitations, prophetic messages, and supernatural signs rare or common in Scripture?
5. How ought we to interact with modern believers who claim that they receive supernatural revelation on a regular basis?

Chapter 3

1. What kind of evidence is most often given in favor of the contemporary view by those who hold to this position?
2. What signs or methodologies are looked to by contemporary view advocates in order to discern the will of God?
3. Why are personal peace and supernatural signs often given disproportionate weight by those who hold to the contemporary view?
4. How can someone best argue for the existence of an individual will of God, that is separate from and more specific than God's moral will and His sovereign will?
5. What challenges and limitations have been raised against the contemporary view? Which challenges do you find to be the most significant?

Chapter 4

1. How do advocates of the traditional view define the individual will of God? How does this differ from advocates of the contemporary view?
2. Is there any situation or topic in life that is not addressed by the moral will of God as it is revealed in Scripture?

3. How would you define biblical wisdom? How does wisdom fit within the traditional view of knowing and doing the will of God?

4. What is a definition of providence? How does providence differ from the sovereign will of God? What things in life are providential?

5. What are some steps that an advocate of the traditional view would take in order to discern the will of God?

Chapter 5

1. What differences exist between contemporary and traditional view advocates regarding the doctrines of prayer, the Holy Spirit, and Christian liberty?

2. Is prayer primarily about revelation or sanctification? Is prayer best described as an opportunity to commune with God or to communicate with God?

3. What is the primarily role of the Holy Spirit in the life of a Christian? What are some secondary roles of the Holy Spirit in a believer's life?

4. Does Christian liberty mean that morality is subjective? How can we winsomely interact with weaker and stronger brethren?

5. What is the role of one's conscience in moral decision making? Does every person have a conscience?

Chapter 6

1. Why do some believers gravitate toward supernatural events, while failing to personally engage in in-depth Bible study?

2. How can we best interact with someone who claims to be a Christian, yet who shows no interest in knowing the will of God?

3. What are some practical steps we can take in order to add depth to our knowledge of the Bible?
4. In the past, have you been clear in the language you've used as you've talked about the will of God?
5. After reading this book, what is your view of how to know and to do the will of God? Has this book changed the way you think about this topic?

ABOUT THE AUTHOR

David W. Jones is a professor and author working in the field of Christian ethics. Dr. Jones is currently serving as Professor of Christian Ethics, Associate Dean of Theological Studies, and Associate Dean of Faculty Support at Southeastern Baptist Theological Seminary (Wake Forest, NC) where he has been teaching since 2001. Dr. Jones holds a B.S. in pastoral ministries, a M.Div. in pastoral ministry, and a Ph.D. in theological studies with an emphasis in Christian ethics. Dr. Jones' scholarly interests include biblical ethics, material stewardship, and topics related to marriage and family life. Dr. Jones serves as a Fellow at the L. Russ Bush Center for Faith & Culture, and has served as a Research Fellow in Christian Ethics at the SBC Ethics & Religious Liberty Commission.

Dr. Jones is the author of many books, articles, essays, and reviews that have appeared in various academic journals as well as in other scholarly publications and in popular venues. His literary works have been translated into numerous foreign languages. Dr. Jones is a moral consultant and is a regular speaker at academic conferences, professional society meetings, radio and television shows, churches, camps, and other ministry-related events. Additionally, Dr. Jones has experience in pastoral and church-planting ministry, denominational work, as well as Bible teaching and curriculum design. He has served as Associate Editor of *The Journal for Biblical Manhood and Womanhood* and is an article referee for both *The Journal of the Evangelical Theological Society* and for *Southeastern Theological Review*. Dr. Jones also serves as a theological reviewer of manuscripts for a number of Christian publishers. He holds memberships in many theological and ethical organizations.

ENDNOTES

Chapter 1

[1] David W. Jones and Russell S. Woodbridge, *Health, Wealth, and Happiness: Has the Prosperity Gospel Overshadowed the Gospel of Christ?* (Grand Rapids, MI: Kregel, 2011). For readers interested in a shorter, popular level treatment of the prosperity gospel, see David W. Jones and Russell S. Woodbridge, *Health, Wealth, and Happiness: How the Prosperity Gospel Overshadows the Gospel of Christ* (Grand Rapids, MI: Kregel, 2017).

[2] Other terminology for the concept of the sovereign will of God includes: God's decretive will, God's hidden will, God's secret will, God's will of decrees, God's efficient will, God's covenant will, God's irresistible will, or God's determined will, God's ultimate will, God's *voluntas beneplaciti* (will of good pleasure). Various terminology is used in different books on the topic.

[3] Differing terms for the moral will of God used by believers include: God's prescriptive will, God's revealed will, God's will of commands, God's permissive will, God's preceptive will, God's resistible will, God's desired will, God's intentional will, or God's *voluntas signi* (will of good sign).

[4] Other references to God's moral will in the Bible include Mark 3:35 and Eph. 6:6, among many additional passages.

Chapter 2

[1] The idea of God as a Shepherd is one of the most common analogies in Scripture that God uses to communicate His character. Other passages where the word-picture of a shepherd

115

is used of God include: Gen. 49:24; Num. 27:15–17; Ps. 23:1–3; 77:20; 80:1; Ezek. 34:5; Matt. 9:36; John 10:27; Heb. 13:20; 1 Pet. 2:25; 5:4; and Rev. 7:17.

[2] Other passages in the Bible where God is referred to as father include: Deut. 32:6; 2 Sam. 7:14; Ps. 103:13; Isa. 63:16; 64:8; Matt. 6:26; 7:7–11; 28:19; Rom. 1:7; 1 Cor. 1:3; 2 Cor. 1:2; 11:31; Gal. 1:4; Eph. 3:14; and 1 John 3:1.

[3] Passages that condemn divination, either explicitly or implicitly, include: Exod. 22:18; Lev. 19:26; 20:27; Deut. 18:9–14; 1 Sam. 15:23; 2 Chron. 33:5–6; Isa. 2:6; Jer. 27:9–10; Ezek. 12:24; 13:6–7, 20–23; and Mal. 3:5.

[4] Jesus and Paul both taught the ability of false prophets to perform signs and wonders will be a phenomenon in the end-times. See Matt. 24:24; Mark 13:22; 2 Thess. 2:9. See also Deut. 18:20; Ezek. 14:9–11; 22:28.

[5] Note Paul's warning to the Ephesian elders, "I know that after my departure fierce wolves will come in among you, not sparing the flock; and from among your own selves will arise men speaking twisted things, to draw away the disciples after them" (Acts 20:29–30).

[6] Another example of pagans casting lots is Jonah 1:7.

[7] A related, but obscure, pagan methodology of divination, which is only mentioned in the Bible at Hos. 4:12, is the use of a divining rod to discern God's will. Scripture contains no details about how a divining rod was used.

[8] Many of the verses in Scripture that refer to idols or to the fashioning of idols are references to teraphim. Examples of such passages include: Gen. 31:19; Lev. 19:4; Isa. 44:9–10; Ezek. 21:21; Hos. 4:12; Zech. 10:2; 1 Thess. 1:9; and 1 John 5:21.

[9] Many question whether Saul actually communed with Samuel in this passage, or if it might have been a demon. It seems best to view this narrative as a miracle facilitated by God in which Samuel was conjured, for the text clearly states four times that it

was Samuel who appeared (1 Samuel 28:14, 15, 16, 20). Moreover, the conjured being accurately prophesied that Israel would lose their battle with the Philistines and that Saul and his sons would die. Knowledge of the future seems to be limited to God and outside the realm of the demonic.

[10] A good question is, "Who killed King Saul?" This is an interesting inquiry, for the Bible teaches that Saul took his own life (see 1 Sam. 31:4–5), that an Amalekite killed Saul (see 2 Sam. 1:10), and that the Philistines killed Saul (see 2 Sam. 21:12). The answer to the question, of course, is that God killed Saul (see 1 Chron. 10:14).

[11] Passages that contain references to astrology include: 2 Ki. 17:16; Isa. 47:13; Jer. 10:2–3.

[12] This is sometimes referred to as "natural law theory" or "ethical rationalism." For a more in-depth discussion of general revelation, see pp. 30–40 in my book *An Introduction to Biblical Ethics* (Nashville, TN: B&H Academic, 2013).

[13] Examples of passages where we see the created order as a means of God's revelation include: Acts 14:15–17; 17:22–31; Rom. 1:18–20.

[14] Some Christians have sought to retain the idea of prophets being present in the modern church. This is usually done by redefining the office of a prophet as a specialized truth-speaker without any ability to foretell the future. Yet, in light of the New Testament usage of the term, such redefinition seems to be illegitimate. In fact, in the book of Acts the New Testament prophets seem to function just like Old Testament prophets, foretelling famines and the future of God's people. Such New Testament appearances of prophets appear to be limited in Scripture to the apostolic era.

[15] There are some possible, although not detailed, examples of the use of the Urim and Thummim in Scripture at Judg. 1:1; 20:18, 23, 28; 1 Sam. 10:22; 14:41; 23:1–13; 30:7–8; 2 Sam. 5:23.

If some of these citations describe legitimate uses of the Urim and Thummim, it seems that this practice or object was capable of giving more than a "yes" or "no" answer.

[16] The Urim and Thummim are mentioned in conjunction with King Saul at 1 Sam. 28:6. While it is unclear if a priest was present, it is probable that there was no priest present, which is why Saul was unable to receive guidance from the Lord on this occasion. It may be that, as was the case when he lost the kingdom, at 1 Sam. 28:6 Saul was again trying to usurp the role of a priest (see 1 Sam. 13:8–14). Note that Saul had earlier murdered many of the priests of God (see 1 Sam. 22:6–23).

[17] Note the many New Testament passages, especially in the Gospel of John, which speak of Jesus being light and perfection (or truth), including: John 1:4–5, 17; 3:19; 8:12; 9:5; 12:46; 14:6.

[18] It may be permissible for Christians to cast lots, if the nuances of the practice could be discerned, to choose between otherwise equal options. As Proverbs teaches, "The lot puts an end to quarrels and decides between powerful contenders. . . . The lot is cast into the lap, but its every decision is from the LORD" (Prov. 16:33; 18:18). But, then again, if the options are otherwise equal, lot-casting would not be necessary to choose one over the other.

[19] Other significant examples in the Bible of those who had dreams and visions from God include: Abimelech (see Gen. 20:3–7), Pharaoh (see Gen. 41:1–36), an unnamed Midianite soldier (see Judg. 7:13–14), the wise men (see Matt. 2:12), and Pilate's wife (see Matt. 27:19).

[20] Note that there are no examples in Scripture of a believer receiving a dream or vision and then seeking interpretation from another human being.

[21] Others in the Old Testament who experienced angelic visitation include: Hagar (see Gen. 16:7), Lot (see Gen. 19:1–17), Jacob (see Gen. 28:12), Joshua (see Josh. 5:15), Gideon (see

Judg. 6:11–27), Manoah and his wife (see Judg. 13:15–20), Balaam (see Num. 22:22–35), Elisha (see 2 Ki. 6:16–17), David (see 2 Sam. 24:16–17), Shadrach, Meshach, and Abednego (see Dan. 3:25) and Zechariah (see Zech. 2:3).

[22] Other New Testament personalities who were visited by angels include: Jesus (see Matt. 4:11; Luke 22:43), Philip (see Acts 8:26), and Cornelius (see Acts 10:3–8).

[23] Another angelic announcement, not related to a birth, was an angel's announcement to Mary Magdalene and the other Mary of Jesus' resurrection (see Matt. 28:5–7).

[24] Note Paul's teaching on the inappropriateness of worshipping angels at Col. 2:18. Also, observe that having great fear and falling prostrate is a common reaction in the Bible when mankind is exposed to the supernatural (see Ezek. 1:28; Dan. 7:15, 28; 8:27; Luke 5:8; Acts 9:4; Rev. 1:17).

[25] It is interesting that when angels appear in Scripture, they are always male in gender, have either no wings or six wings (Isa. 6:2), and speak the language of those with whom they come in contact. Clearly, many artists' conception of angels as being little children or female with two wings is incorrect.

[26] Another unique example of man asking for a sign and God accommodating the request is Jonathan's request in 1 Sam. 14:6–10. This appears to be a one-time event in Jonathan's life.

[27] One of the rare examples of a sign being requested, in a positive manner, is David's desire for a sign of favor at Ps. 86:17.

[28] Note Matthew's later commentary about Jesus' limited ministry in His hometown of Nazareth, "And he did not do many mighty works there, because of their unbelief" (Matt. 13:58).

Chapter 3

[1] Other writers have labeled this the majority view or the

traditional view. Majority view is an accurate description, as many Western Christians hold this view today; however, traditional view is a misnomer, for this perspective is not the traditional view of the church.

[2] Examples of Christians who espouse the contemporary view include: Henry Blackaby and Claude King, *Experiencing God: Knowing and Doing the Will of God* (Nashville: B&H, 2008); Tim LaHaye, *Finding the Will of God in a Crazy, Mixed-Up World* (Grand Rapids: Zondervan, 1989); Jack Deere, *Surprised by the Voice of God* (Grand Rapids: Zondervan, 1998); and Kenneth Hagin, *How You Can Know the Will of God* (1989).

[3] See the resources in the previous endnote for a more detailed explanation of how advocates of this position apply this view to decision-making.

[4] It is worth noting that there are no biblical examples of an individual claiming adherence to God's individual will as a rationale for a choice, decision, or course of action. Note further that there are no examples in Scripture of anyone actively seeking God's individual will via direct communication from God after Acts 1:24–26, which was the choosing of Matthias as an apostle. This is possibly explained by the bestowal of the Holy Spirit at Pentecost.

[5] For more on the naturalistic fallacy see my discussion in David W. Jones, *An Introduction to Biblical Ethics* (Nashville: B&H, 2013), 38.

[6] This scenario highlights another shortcoming of the contemporary view—that is, many of the means of revelation used to discern God's will are inherently unverifiable.

[7] This is not to say material human flourishing, or even a desire for such, is sinful. Rather, it is when material prosperity becomes an idol that it becomes sinful.

[8] This actually is an insufficient example, but I am trying to give an illustration similar to the way in which people use this view.

The example is insufficient, for all job offers come with salary arrangements; thus, looking at a salary range is not a supernatural sign at all. Rather, it is a circumstantial sign. Gideon's sign of the fleece being wet or dry was truly a supernatural event, for the morning dew falls equally on all things. For the fleece to be wet or to be dry was not circumstantial but was a miracle.

Chapter 4

[1] Different authors have assigned various names to the traditional view, including the character view, the wisdom view, and the relational view.

[2] Examples of books that adopt the traditional view include: Kevin DeYoung, *Just Do Something: A Liberating Approach to Finding God's Will* (Chicago: Moody, 2014); Garry Friesen, *Decision Making and the Will of God* (Eugene, OR: Multnomah, 2009); John MacArthur, *Found: God's Will* (Colorado Springs: David C. Cook, 2012); and Bruce Waltke, *Finding the Will of God: A Pagan Notion?* (Grand Rapids: Eerdmans, 2002). Note that I give a number of books in the suggested reading list at the conclusion of this volume, all of which espouse the traditional view.

[3] Note Paul's exhortation to "understand what the will of the Lord is" (Eph. 5:17). This shows that God's will is to be driven by understanding and knowledge, not primarily by emotion and experience.

[4] At Phil. 2:5 Paul exhorts his readers to have the mind of Christ. There is a similar teaching at 1 Pet. 4:1. In light of these exhortations, many believers wonder how to gain the mind of Christ, with some advocates of the contemporary view teaching that it must be developed mystically via extra-biblical revelation. Yet, at 1 Cor. 2:16 Paul taught his readers, "We have the mind of Christ." Contextually, it is clear that Paul is referring to the Word of God. Since the Bible is God's self-revelation, it reveals His

mind.

[5] This pattern can be seen throughout church history, as well as in Scripture. For example, in Acts 15:23–29, the Jerusalem council justified their decision to send Judas and Silas to deliver their ruling, along with Paul and Barnabas, simply because "it has seemed good to us" (Acts 15:25). This was just a wise decision in light of the churches' need to be able to verify the truth of Paul and Barnabas' message. Another instance is the apostles' wise decision to appoint deacons in the early church in light of the possible unequal distribution of food (see Acts 6:1–5).

[6] This is an important caveat. To define human flourishing by the standards of mankind opens the door to the prosperity gospel.

[7] Note Jesus' teaching, "Come to Me all you who labor and are heavy laden, and I will give you rest. Take My yoke on you and learn of Me, for I am meek and lowly in heart, and you shall find rest to your souls. For My yoke is easy, and My burden is light" (Matt. 11:28–30).

[8] For a more in-depth treatment of this idea, see my book: David W. Jones, *An Introduction to Biblical Ethics* (Nashville: B&H Academic, 2013), 40–51.

[9] The written Word of God (i.e., the Bible) and the living Word of God (i.e., Jesus Christ) reveal the same quantity—that is, God's moral will.

[10] There are, of course, many things that God cannot do, all of which relate to His character. These include: lie (cf. Titus 1:2; Heb. 6:18), break His covenants (cf. Ps. 89:34), change (cf. Mal. 3:6), repent (cf. Num. 23:19), be unjust (cf. Exod. 34:7), tire (cf. Isa 40:28), deny Himself (cf. 2 Tim. 2:13), reject the elect (cf. John 6:37), and share His glory (cf. Isa. 42:8), among many other things that are revealed in Scripture.

[11] For my fuller treatment of general revelation, see Jones, *An*

Introduction to Biblical Ethics, 30–40.

[12] I've written more extensively on the doctrine of work, as well as the ethics of wealth and poverty, in David W. Jones, *Every Good Thing: An Introduction to the Material World and the Common Good for Christians* (Bellingham, WA: Lexham Press, 2016).

[13] God's knowledge actually extends beyond His sovereign will. God not only knows what has happened, what is happening, and what will happen, but also what could have happened. This concept, called exhaustive divine foreknowledge, is evident in passages such as 1 Sam. 23:11–12 where God reveals the unrealized but true betrayal of David by the inhabitants of Keilah. This concept is also present in Jesus' teaching about the unrealized but true repentance of Tyre, Sidon, and Sodom that would have occurred if they had received the witness of the Galilean ministry of Jesus (see Matt. 11:21–24).

[14] In his 1692 book *A Body of Divinity* Puritan writer Thomas Watson helpfully observed, "Providence is a Christian's diary, not his Bible." Thomas Watson, *A Body of Divinity* (Carlisle, PA: Banner of Truth, 1958), 123.

[15] A further Old Testament example related to reading providence is that of Queen Esther. When God's people were in danger of extermination at the hands of Haman, Mordecai rhetorically asked Esther, "And who knows whether you have not come to the kingdom for such a time as this?" (Est. 4:14). In other words, Mordecai *suggests* that God had providentially put Esther into a position of power, but he cannot be *certain*. What was sure was that for Esther to not act would have been a violation of the moral law. A biblical example where the error of reading providence can be seen is in Micah's incorrect assumption that the appearance of a Levite was proof that God would bless his idolatry (see Judg. 17:13).

[16] In the New Testament, too, Jesus warned His hearers about attempting to read providence (see Luke 13:1–5; John 9:1–3).

[17] Another example from Paul's ministry is his going to Jerusalem despite being begged by believers not to go, for they knew he would be persecuted there (see Acts 21:4, 10–11). These well-meaning Christians assumed that since trials awaited Paul in Jerusalem, then he should not travel there. Yet, Paul testified that he was being compelled by the Holy Spirt (see Acts 19:21; 20:22) and fulfilling the ministry of Christ (see Acts 20:24) by traveling to Jerusalem. Paul knew that he could not read providence based upon blessings and suffering in the world. His mission was to follow God's moral will, which had been revealed to him and was not dependent upon nor determined by the circumstances.

[18] The penitential psalms are 6, 32, 38, 51, 102, 130, and 143.

[19] The Hebrew term translated "paths" occurs thirty-four times in Psalms and Proverbs: Ps. 8:8; 16:11; 17:4; 19:5; 25:4, 10; 27:11; 44:18; 119:9, 15, 101, 104, 128; 139:3; 142:3; Prov. 1:19; 2:8, 13, 15, 19, 20; 3:6; 4:14, 18; 5:6; 8:20; 9:15; 10:17; 12:28; 15:10, 19; 15:24; 17:23; 22:25.

[20] Parallels in Pauline usage of the terms "good," "acceptable," and "perfect" also suggest that Paul is referring to God's moral will in Rom. 12:2 (see Rom. 7:12).

[21] In regard to the moral will of God, Scripture teaches that the duties of a pastor include: shepherding and being an example to the flock (see 1 Pet. 5:2), exhorting others in sound doctrine (see Titus 1:9), and "equipping of the saints for the work of ministry" (Eph. 4:12).

Chapter 5

[1] Note Jesus' teaching that through prayer believers can move mountains (see Mark 11:20–24). Of course, Christ is speaking metaphorically in this passage. Yet, saving faith, which seems to be Jesus' focus in this passage, is greater than moving mountains.

[2] In his excellent book on prayer, Tim Keller captures this idea

well as he writes, "Without immersion in God's words, our prayers may not be merely limited and shallow but untethered from reality. . . . Without prayer that answers the God of the Bible, we will only be talking to ourselves. . . . The lesson here is not that God never guides our thoughts or prompts us to choose a wise course of action, but that we cannot be *sure* he is speaking to us unless we read it in the Scripture." Tim Keller, *Prayer: Experiencing Awe and Intimacy with God* (New York: Penguin, 2014), 62–63.

3 By way of example, note Jesus' prayer in the Garden of Gethsemane. Christ prayed, "Not as I will, but as you will" (Matt. 26:39).

4 When our prayers are unanswered in the way we desire, we can be comforted in knowing that we are in good company. Jesus prayed three times for the cup of God's wrath to be removed from Him, but it was not (see Matt. 26:36–46), and Paul prayed three times for the thorn in his flesh to be removed, but it was not (see 2 Cor. 12:7–10). Note that on each of these occasions Jesus and Paul were submissive to God's sovereign will.

5 Jesus taught that persistence in prayer is also important, for our persistence demonstrates that God's will is important to us, as it is to Him (see Luke 11:5–10; 18:1–8). Three reasons why persistence in prayer is helpful: (1) it fosters dependence upon God; (2) it causes us to examine our requests; and (3) it purges and shapes our requests to be more God-focused.

6 For more on the concept of praying in Jesus' name, see Jones, *An Introduction to Biblical Ethics*, 159–160.

7 Other examples of the Holy Spirit directly revealing God's will in the book of Acts include the Holy Spirit's guidance of the Jerusalem Council (see Acts 15:28), as well as numerous times during Paul's ministry (see Acts 16:6–7; 20:22–23).

8 Note Paul's similar teaching, as he asserted, "Now we have received not the spirit of the world, but the Spirit who is from

God, that we might understand the things freely given us by God. And we impart this in words not taught by human wisdom but taught by the Spirit, interpreting spiritual truths to those who are spiritual" (1 Cor. 2:12–13).

[9] This can be most clearly seen in Paul's parallel use of the phrases "be filled with the Spirit" (Eph. 5:18) and "Let the word of Christ dwell in you richly" (Col. 3:16).

[10] Additional passages that mention the Holy Spirit and divine peace include: Acts 9:31; Rom. 14:17; 15:13; Eph. 4:3; and 1 Pet. 1:2.

[11] For more information on the essential components of a moral event, see Jones, *An Introduction to Biblical Ethics*, 1–27.

[12] Other key passages that address Christian liberty include: 1 Cor. 6:12; Gal. 5:13; and Col. 3:17.

[13] While sometimes used to describe individuals who maintain a loose connection with the church, the idea of a "carnal Christian" is questionable, at best. Although it is certainly possible to backslide for a short season of time, Jesus taught that there will be many who have knowledge of Christ but are not truly regenerate. According to Jesus, the way to tell the difference between an unregenerate "carnal Christian" and a true follower of Christ is, "You will recognize them by their fruits" (Matt. 7:16).

[14] We ought not to confuse a weaker brother with a so-called "professional weaker brother." A professional weaker brother is someone, like the Pharisees in the Gospel narratives, who attempts to manipulate others to conform to their own extra-biblical moral scruples. At Matt. 15:14 Jesus' instructions concerning such foolish individuals are clear, "Let them alone; they are blind guides. And if the blind lead the blind, both will fall into a pit" (see Prov. 9:7; 16:22; 23:9; 26:4; 29:9; Matt. 7:6; Titus 3:10).

[15] This is not to say that stronger brethren disregard the moral

law. Rather, mature believers have a transformed mind such that they desire to keep God's moral law, realizing that it is the only way to true freedom. Bear in mind the fact that true freedom is not the opportunity to do whatever one wants; rather, it is the ability to do what one is designed to do.

SCRIPTURE INDEX

GENERAL INDEX

Made in the USA
Columbia, SC
16 December 2021

51580755R00095